# The Same, But Different

# The Same, But Different

## Ministry and the Quaker Pastor

By Phil Baisley

Friends United Press

Friends United Press
101 Quaker Hill Drive
Richmond, IN 47374
info@fum.org
friendsunitedmeeting.org


Library of Congress Cataloging-in-Publication Data

Author: Baisley, Philip C., 1952–.
Title: The same but different : ministry and the quaker pastor / by Philip C. Baisley.
Description: First [edition]. | Richmond, Indiana : Friends United Press, 2018.
Identifiers: LCCN 2018002793| ISBN 9780913408698 (pbk.) | ISBN 9780913408735 (hardcover)
Subjects: LCSH: Society of Friends--Clergy. | Pastoral theology--Society of Friends.
Classification: LCC BX7745 .B325 2018 | DDC 262/.1496--dc23 LC record available at https://lccn.loc.gov/2018002793

# CONTENTS

# ACKNOWLEDGMENTS

**M**any years ago, I attempted to design a seminary course specifically for Friends pastors. I searched for a textbook. The closest thing I found was Samuel Bownas' classic, *A Description of the Qualifications Necessary to a Gospel Minister*. That book was written in 1750; and, although it still has much to say in the twenty-first century, and I use it occasionally in classes and workshops, I really hoped something newer would be available. In lieu of a single text, I drew from multiple sources that included "Quakerly" ideas but were not written by Quakers. From then on, I set out to write this book.

Support for writing came in three tiers. Since the initial study that produced the data on which this book is based came from my Doctor of Ministry dissertation, Tier One consists of my dissertation advisors, the late Dr. Luke Keefer of Ashland Theological Seminary and Dr. Stephen Angell at Earlham School of Religion. They stuck with me from the beginning, through a leave of absence due to my parents' ill health and deaths, and they remained until the bitter end. Without their encouragement for the research that produced the "why" and "what" of Quaker pastoral ministry, this book would not have been written.

Tier Two included the people who read, edited, pushed, and shoved me toward completion. First, my readers: Katie Ubry-Terrell (my 2BF), Quaker historians Tom Hamm and Steve Angell, friend and Friend Della Stanley-Green, and my son Stephen Baisley. Second, the pastors and friends who shared their stories with me and allowed me to include them here. Finally, a big THANK YOU to my editor at Friends United Press, Kristna Evans. We didn't always agree, but we found ways to collaborate.

Tier Three were those people who inspire me to write whatever I write. First among these is the best wife in the world (it says so on my phone every time she calls), Jennifer Brokamp. She actually believes in me, for which I will be forever grateful. Other family members pushed me at appropriate times. I'll thank my son, Stephen, again here, and also my daughter, Kellyn. Their mom, Sandy, always supported this project as well. Last, but not least, is the guy who never stopped believing that I'd finish this book, and who remains convinced it just might be necessary: former dean of Earlham School of Religion, Jay Marshall.

Thanks be to God for bringing these wonderful folks into my life.

*For my parents, Fran and Art Baisley,*
*who taught me most of the important stuff*
*about ministry.*

# INTRODUCTION

One fall day, some years ago, an acquaintance asked me to give the invocation at a scholarship awards banquet hosted by the Indiana Football Hall of Fame. After the dinner and a speech by a college coach, five boys were to receive scholarships based on their academic and athletic prowess. My part, according to the Hall of Fame board member who invited me, was to offer a blessing before the meal. Pretty straightforward and simple. As pastors we have to do things like that from time to time. We may debate within our minds whether to pray according to our own beliefs, or to pray a "generic" prayer inclusive of those whose beliefs may differ from ours. We may question the whole idea of praying at a secular event, but mostly we do it because we're "the pastor."

Not being one to turn down a free meal catered by an area-renowned barbecue specialist, I agreed to give the invocation. Knowing, generally, the audience, I composed a brief Christian prayer of thankfulness for God's presence, appreciation for the benefits of high school sports, and a blessing for the food to be served and for those who prepared it. I wrote it all on an index card that fit neatly in my pocket.

Everything went beautifully. If you are a pastor, you know the joy of praying just the right prayer for an occasion. I moved through the serving line hearing words of appreciation from many of the coaches and parents at the banquet. "Nice prayer, Preacher," always makes us feel good. The food was amazing. The speaker was entertaining. When the time came for the scholarships to be presented, I was proud to live in a state that could produce such high-caliber student athletes.

It was during the presentations when the board chairperson whispered to me, "That was a great invocation. Could you have another prayer at the end?" I nodded my head while thinking, "Oh, crap! I'm out of index cards, and I don't have a pen." I recalled the advice of a Bible college professor, "A minister of the Gospel should always be ready to pray, preach, or die." Well, I did have a sermon outline or two in my wallet, and death didn't seem like such a bad idea right then. I just wasn't sure about the prayer part. Another general kind of prayer would seem phony. And I didn't know enough about the honorees to pray specifically for them. So I played the "Quaker card."

There really isn't a Quaker card. Okay, I do carry a card signifying that I have ministry gifts that have been recognized by a regional body of Friends, but I don't actually use it for anything. What I did was fall back on a part of ministry that seems distinctly Quaker, although we don't own the copyright.

When the scholarships were handed out, and all five boys were duly honored, the board chairperson re-introduced me. I'm sure everyone in the hall was expecting another prayer. It would have been so easy, even though I might have felt a little uncomfortable. A lot of pastors I've known would have prayed, said "Amen," and gone home happy. Instead, I told the group that I'd been asked to close the festivities, but I hadn't been sure how best to do that. Then I remembered the Quaker idea of "holding a person in the Light." I described it as a way of blessing that person. I said we would all be quiet for a few moments and that I would say the name of each honoree. After each name

I would pause, allowing anyone or everyone present to offer their own prayer or blessing or kind thought for that boy. One by one I said the names, paused to enjoy the silent blessings, and concluded with an "Amen." Afterward, the parents of each of the five boys said nothing could have been more meaningful.

Why did I do that? Where did I come up with the audacity not to pray when everyone expected me to pray? Why could I not have left well enough alone? Because I'm a Friends pastor. Because I believe there is something to the idea that God is present in a gathering like that, and God doesn't need my eloquence to make it meaningful. In those final banquet moments, a whole room full of men and women ministered to five high school football players. I was just there doing what Quakers try to do: get out of the way of the Spirit.

I've been connected to the Society of Friends, also known as Quakers (I'll use the terms interchangeably), for over thirty years, spending some time with unprogrammed Friends—the ones without pastors or formal orders of worship—but mostly among Friends of the programmed, or pastoral, variety. I've been a Friends pastor and known dozens more, and I've often wondered whether Quaker pastors are the same as, or different from, other pastors.

Think about it: They preach. They teach. They celebrate happy and sad and tragic moments with families and strangers. They share the Good News, and they sit in interminably long committee meetings. It certainly seems like they're the same as every pastor in town. But are they also different? Are Quaker pastors different from, say, the Baptist pastor down the street, the Presbyterian minister across town, or the local Catholic priest? If so, how are they different?

Some years ago I researched that question. I surveyed Friends pastors, denominational leaders, and educators, and I learned that, for the most part, people involved in Quaker pastoral ministry believe there is something unique about the way they envision and practice ministry. They see the Quaker pastor as the same, but also different from other clergy, and they relate that difference to some foundational principles. At the same time, as I presented my findings to Friends (capital F, meaning other Quakers) and also to friends who were not Quakers, I started hearing that these foundational principles are not just for Quakers. They appear in various expressions in the ministers' manuals and books of discipline of many churches. Again it seems we Quaker pastors are the same, but different.

My experience as a Friends pastor, an educator in other denominations, and a member or attender in churches from Anabaptist to Wesleyan (couldn't think of an X, Y, or Z), taught me that Friends may be more intentional about practicing some of the specifics that most Christians believe. They create opportunities where ministry is more than just the work of the clergy. They fully expect worship to be led by the Spirit and not just the worship team. But they don't have a monopoly on these things.

In writing this book I have two aims. I want to encourage Friends pastors to unashamedly practice their faith according to Quaker traditions. Those traditions are grounded in scripture as well as nearly four centuries of experience, and they guide us toward a different way of doing ministry. I also want to show readers from other faith traditions what happens when our mutual foundational beliefs are carried out in the everyday work of local pastors. The way I hope these things will happen is through stories: stories I've heard and stories I've lived.

Getting to those stories will require a little background. So this book will begin with a brief history of how some Friends came to embrace, or at least tolerate, pastors. Following that history, I will describe how some of Friends' theological foundations form the Quaker pastor and inform Quaker pastoral ministry. Once the historical and theological bases are covered, we'll go on to some traditional pastoral practices that Quaker pastors see and do a little differently than other pastors. That's where I'll tell the stories I've heard and lived. I hope you will identify with these stories, whether or not you are a Friend. And I hope you will walk with me until the end of this journey, where we will consider some implications that this "same but different" way of doing ministry may have for our future as pastors, whether we are Friends or friends.

# ▪ 1 ▪

## Where Do Quaker Pastors Come From?

One evening, so the story goes, a little boy jumped onto his father's lap and asked the dreaded question, "Where do I come from?" The father hemmed and hawed, hoping the child would lose interest before he had to respond. It didn't work. Finally, the father explained in great detail how babies are made. "Wow," said the boy, "Jessie said she came from Peoria."

Explaining the advent of Friends pastors can feel nearly as lengthy and awkward as the father's experience in this little anecdote. Quakers haven't always had pastors. For a long time in their history, the Society of Friends, which believes all people are ministers, frowned upon anyone receiving pay for regularly ministering in their meetings. However, in little more than a century, Friends went from having no pastors to their present state where there are more Friends meetings (churches) with pastors than without. How did this happen? Where did all those Quaker pastors come from?

The Society of Friends began in mid-seventeenth century England. This was a time of religious fervor in England as Puritans attempted to reform the Church of England and dozens of radical religious groups vied for the allegiance of the people. These radical groups proved to be fertile ground for a movement begun by a young man disillusioned with established English religion, George Fox.

George Fox was born in Drayton-in-the-Clay, Leicestershire, in 1624.[1] As a young person he became disenchanted with both the Church of England and the Puritans. In his journal, Fox describes his spiritual quest in great detail, culminating in a revelation of Jesus Christ:

> Now after I had received that opening from the Lord that to be bred at Oxford or Cambridge was not sufficient to fit a man to be a minister of Christ, I regarded the priests less, and looked more after the dissenting people. And among them I saw there was some tenderness, and many of them came afterwards to be convinced, for they had some openings. But as I had forsaken all the priests, so I left the separate preachers also, and those called the most experienced people; for I saw there was none among them all that could speak to my condition. And when all my hopes in them and in all men were gone, so that I had nothing outwardly to help me, nor could I tell what to do, then, Oh, then, I heard a voice which said, "There is one, even Christ Jesus, that can speak to thy condition," and when I heard it my heart did leap for joy. Then the Lord did let me see why there was none upon the earth that could speak to my condition, namely, that I might give Him all the glory.[2]

Fox's words do more than describe a personal religious experience. They provide the foundation for the Quaker belief that people do not need a priest or preacher to mediate the word of God to them. Later in his *Journal*, Fox goes on to write of his conviction "that the Lord Christ Jesus was come to teach his people himself and bring them off all the world's ways and teachers to Christ, their way to God."[3] It requires no stretch of the imagination, then, to understand why Friends saw no need for paid pastors during their first two centuries.

In spite of their implicit rejection of professional clergy, early Friends recognized that there were ministers in their meetings. Elton Trueblood notes in *The People Called Quakers*,

Of all the mistaken notions about Quakers, the most extreme is the supposition that they have no ministers. The misunderstanding on this important point is so widespread that it is actually grotesque. In the beginning of the Movement the fact that a large proportion of the members, of both sexes, were clearly engaged in the ministry, was perhaps, from the point of view of the outside observer, the most striking single feature of Quaker life. Not only were the rank and file of the members ministers in the sense that they performed humble services to their fellow men in daily life; many of them were also ministers in the sense that they preached wherever and whenever they could.[4]

The following story from *The Journal of the Life of William Edmundson* is one of many examples of individuals ministering whenever it seemed God asked it of them:

The next day I came to Londonderry; it was market-day, and there were stage-players and rope-dancers in the market-place, and abundance of people gathered. The Lord's Spirit filled my heart, his power struck at them, and his word was sharp. So I stood in the market-place, and proclaimed the day of the Lord among them, and warned them all to repent. The dread of the Almighty came over them, and they were as people amazed. When I found my spirit a little eased, I walked along the street, and the people flocked about me, I found my spirit drawn forth towards them. I stood still and declared truth to them, directing them to the light of Christ in their own hearts, and they were very sober and attentive.[5]

Such stories of vocal ministry among early Friends seem to focus on preaching in the marketplace or in Anglican churches, Puritan meetings, and other religious gatherings. But what happened during the meetings Friends held among themselves?

From their beginning in the 1650s to the late nineteenth century, Friends meetings tended to be characterized by silence or, more appropriately, by waiting. Hugh Barbour describes this form of worship as a group sitting "in an unadorned room in silence of mind and body 'waiting upon God' until one or more members feel led by the Spirit to speak or pray."[6]

Because Friends believed so strongly in the immediate presence of God in their meetings, any advance preparation of a message was forbidden. Thomas Hamm sums up the Quaker view of speaking in worship as follows:

Since preaching or other ministry had to be done under the immediate inspiration of the Holy Spirit, Friends forbade any form of preparation. Even to bring along a Bible to read in meeting was rare. Ministers had no professional status. They worked at secular employment to support themselves. And they took the silent waiting as seriously as any other member. It was not uncommon for a minister to ask Friends to hold a special meeting and then to sit silent throughout it.[7]

In spite of the egalitarian nature of Friends' ministry, even in the movement's earliest days some people were singled out as having been given a special gift of ministry. Some of these ministered in the world at large, as was the case with Fox, Edmundson, and many other men and women; and some ministered in their local meeting. It was in the context of local ministry that some comparison might be drawn with pastoral work, and yet a distinction must be made. Unlike a church that calls a minister and expects regular duties to be performed, early Friends ministers felt they were called by God with no expectation upon them but to be obedient to God's leading. Whether they stayed at their home meeting or journeyed to other meetings, these ministers sought only to be faithful.

This acknowledgement of special gifts led to meetings formally recognizing the ministry of these persons by "recording" their ministry gift. Thomas Hamm explains that "the word *record* is important. Human beings could only recognize a gift bestowed by God. They could not advance it, nor could any human act, such as ordination, bestow special power or legitimacy on it."[8]

Although no preparation for the message was thought to be necessary by Friends, and no formal preparation was required for the minister, Friends were quite clear on the spiritual preparation needed before a man or woman could be considered qualified for doing vocal ministry. The most thorough description of this kind of preparation is given by Samuel Bownas in his book, *A Description of the Qualifications Necessary to a Gospel Minister*. First, Bownas emphasizes the spirituality of the minister by saying,

> There must be a state of sanctification (in degree) known, by the spirit of judgment and burning, before any can be proper objects to be receivers of this inspiring gift, that can only assist a minister, and make him instrumental of doing good to others. The tree must be good, before the fruit can be so; and right and true ministers are to be known by their fruits.[9]

Bownas goes on to declare that ministers who are in a proper relationship with God are qualified to speak from their own experience of the power of God in their lives:

> This preparation by the Spirit for the ministry so qualifies the receiver of this excellent inspiring gift, when called to the work, that he can experimentally say, "What I have tasted, felt, and heard of the good word of life, and the powers of the world to come, I declare unto you."[10]

The authority given to personal experience as a basis for ministry stems from the belief that the Spirit who inspired the biblical writers is presently active among people.

While Friends paid meticulous attention to the spiritual qualifications for ministers throughout their first two hundred years of history, any thought of what we might call "practical" preparation for ministers was discouraged. Friends were fond of reminding themselves of George Fox's words regarding higher education:

> At another time, as I was walking in a field on a First-day morning, the Lord opened unto me that being bred at Oxford or Cambridge was not enough to fit and qualify men to be ministers of Christ; and I stranged at it because it was the common belief of people.[11]

A great change began taking place among American Friends in the latter part of the nineteenth century. Throughout the 1800s, many Friends in the American Midwest were identifying more and more with the revivals sweeping that part of the country. Some of these revivals were connected to the preaching of people like Charles Finney, while others arose spontaneously after lengthy prayer meetings.

Thomas Hamm, in *The Transformation of American Quakerism*, does an excellent job pointing out the reasons why so many American Friends embraced the holiness movement, and the purpose of this chapter is not to justify or condemn Friends' actions. However, the holiness doctrine did attract a great many to Friends and this, in turn, brought about a situation Friends had not experienced before and were ill-prepared to deal with effectively: numeric growth, particularly among people who had not been Friends. About this influx of non-Quakers, Hamm writes:

> The revival, of course, was not aimed solely at those who were already Quakers; the hundreds of new members that the revivals brought in posed the greatest problem for the society. Some were former Friends who had in the past fallen victim to the discipline, but many were strangers to Quaker tradition. All had been converted in a setting that was very different from the traditional Quaker meeting. The worship of Friends seemed utterly foreign to many, since as late as the 1880s most meetings were unprogrammed. Some converts took advantage of the silence to unburden their consciences in unseemly ways, and others insisted on singing hymns. Trying to hold these new members in the society would give rise to even more radical innovations in the 1880s.[12]

To give an idea of how great this influx of new converts was, Indiana Yearly Meeting had a fifty percent increase in membership between 1881 and 1889. During the revival era, it was not unusual for a Friends meeting to have as many people seeking membership as it already had on its membership rolls. One Midwestern county, Van Wert in Ohio, went from having no resident Friends in 1875 to having nearly a thousand Friends spread among seven meetings in 1890.[13]

The question on the minds of many American Friends in the late nineteenth century concerned what to do with all the new people attending and joining their meetings. How would they learn the value of silence when all they had known previously was revival preaching? Who would guide their movement from inward spiritual transformation toward the outward manifestations of that transformation in their behavior and actions in the world (as opposed to focusing on salvation and the afterlife)?

In theory, Friends had a system in place for dealing with new members. It was accomplished through the meeting community itself. When a new person or family would begin an association with Friends, the local meeting would informally instruct them in Friends' beliefs and practices. This worked well when new converts entered the meeting one family at a time. While it was the community's responsibility to disciple them, usually an elder or two would make the effort. However, as new attenders came by the dozens, the system broke down. Everyone's responsibility often became no one's responsibility, and converts slipped through the proverbial cracks, drifting away from the uncomfortable silence and the unexplained ways of Friends.

This probably sounds foreign to you, doesn't it? Unless you were brought up in the unprogrammed Friends tradition, it is likely you are having trouble relating to the depth of the dilemma those Midwestern Friends faced. Maybe if we put ourselves in the position of the new converts, we might understand it better.

I have a number of friends who love Zumba, that frenzied dance-exercise program. They say anyone can do it, and I'm sure that's true. However, the only time I ever tried it was as part of a kind of mass Zumba experience at the county fairgrounds. There were dozens of us in an outdoor pavilion. I was excited about joining the fun. The thing is, almost everyone there was a regular Zumba practitioner. There was a whole row of instructors in front of us, and they were moving so fast I couldn't keep up. The people around me didn't seem to notice me floundering around—yes, I'm sure I looked like a flounder out of water—as they went through what was for them a well-known routine.

Now what if I weren't the only uninitiated Zumba-ist (Zumbie?) at the event. What if you and one hundred others were there among the forty or fifty fitness dancers? We'd jump in enthusiastically, try really hard, and then slowly drop toward the back of the pavilion as we realized we were unable to participate fully in this thing we so wanted to join. We'd watch from the edges, shaking a leg here or there, wishing we could figure it out. Eventually, one by one, we'd leave the group and go get a lemon shake-up.

"Preposterous!" Zumba aficionados will say. "No Zumba instructor would allow that to happen." But there were many instructors there that day—almost as many instructors as dancers. And no one stood out from the others. Everyone was already well versed in Zumba routines. You might say, with almost everyone being an instructor, no one was an instructor. And the uninitiated, meaning you and I, quietly went away. Now imagine we're talking church and not Zumba.

Friends became concerned about both the influx of new members and the purity of the existing Society. Some suggested a probation and observation period before membership. Others created pastoral committees to instruct new converts in Friends' ways. By 1885, the idea of the pastoral committee was widespread, but another idea was sweeping through the meetings most influenced by the revivals.[14]

Although Friends had always had persons in their meetings who were gifted in and regularly exercised pastoral gifts, the setting apart of someone for professional pastoral ministry was foreign to Quakers. One reason may have had to do with the responsibility for delivering a weekly sermon or message. Friends had traditionally looked to God for the message and expected it to come through anyone God chose, although some persons were recognized (recorded) as regular channels for such vocal ministry. The revivals, however, resulted in more emphasis on preaching. After all, it was the preaching of the revivalists that inspired the converts.

By the 1890s, many American Friends meetings were engaging persons to do such pastoral activities as preaching and teaching new converts. Since those persons were, in some sense, set apart to do ministries no longer expected of other meeting members, the question of financial remuneration then became an issue.[15] Soon the idea of paid pastors, something akin to the "hireling ministers" earlier Friends had railed against,[16] became the accepted way of revivalist Friends who were forming a significant part of Midwestern American Quakerism.

Pastoral Quakerism had its critics right from the start. In Iowa Yearly Meeting, where the pastoral system seemed to have had its strongest foothold,[17] Joel Bean wrote a scathing article that was published in *The British Friend*, denouncing the movement. He questioned the stance many had taken that pastors were being called to facilitate the instruction of new members and argued that the pastoral system elevated a few ministers while squelching the ministry of others. Bean predicted a downward slide that could easily lead to—horror of horrors—a published order of worship.[18]

In every yearly meeting where pastoral Quakerism took root, there were vocal opponents to the movement. As with Bean in Iowa, the key issues were worship and leadership. Regarding worship, those who rejected a paid pastoral ministry were concerned that meetings would become so programmed that they would lose the concept of "waiting," that preaching and singing and formal prayers would limit or eliminate the silence and expectant waiting on the Spirit that was so dear to early Friends. As for leadership, Bean's image of recorded ministers having "little strength or place to speak" expressed the fear that meeting leadership would become bound up in one person, rather than spread among all meeting members.[19]

In spite of opposition, pastoral Quakerism became a dominant factor in the Society of Friends in parts of the United States, in Latin America, and in East Africa. Sadly, it has been my experience that Bean's and other Friends' misgivings have come true in many places. I have sat in Quaker meetings longing for a moment's respite from the busy-ness, wishing there would be some time for silence so we could hear the Spirit, should the Spirit choose to speak. I have seen meetings where the pastor took on so much responsibility that little ministry was left for the membership to do.

But I have also been in meetings among pro-grammed Friends where the Spirit has gathered us, where we have listened and we have heard a word from God. I've attended meetings where the pastor exercises her gifts as one of many gifted members, encouraging all the meeting to share in the ministry. I do not be-lieve the pastoral system has irreparably damaged the Society of Friends in places where it is practiced. It has, however, created a kind of pastor who looks at ministry from a point of view unlike most ministers. It is a point of view that comes from standing on a foundation deeply rooted in Quaker theology.

# ▪ 2 ▪

## The Presence in the Midst

Hanging somewhere in a hallway, worship room, fellowship hall, or basement of countless Quaker meetinghouses in the United States, Canada, England, and even in places like Kenya and Bolivia, is a painting by an artist named Doyle Penrose. It is called *The Presence in the Midst*, and it depicts a group of Friends gathered in worship at the Jordans Friends Meeting House near London, England. The focus of the painting is not the worshipers; rather it is the spectral presence of the Christ figure standing among them. This is a picture of Quakerism in its rawest form and perhaps the only feature of Quaker doctrine common to Friends the world over—that Christ (or God) is present and active wherever His people gather to worship.

THE PRESENCE IN THE MIDST
*Doyle Penrose*

If you were to ask me what the core belief of Quakers is, I would relate it to their interpretation of that picture. Whether they describe the presence as God or Christ or Spirit or something else would indicate something about their theology. How they feel that presence affects worship, religious education, church business, ministry, and outreach would indicate something about their ecclesiology. I believe the idea of an immediate, active presence of God when the church meets together is the foundational belief that drives Quaker ministry and, in turn, gives the Quaker pastor her unique perspective.

In some ways, *The Presence in the Midst* links Quakers to Roman Catholicism, since Catholics find in the Eucharist the real presence of Christ in their midst, but Quakers are not Catholic. Quakerism may be considered a form of Protestantism, since most Protestants are drawn in worship to the Word of God, which is incarnate in Jesus Christ. But Quakers are not really Protestant either. Howard Brinton contrasts Quaker worship with that of Catholics and Protestants, saying,

> As Catholic worship is centered in the altar and Protestant worship in the sermon, worship for the Society of Friends attempts to realize as its center the divine Presence revealed within. In a Catholic church the altar is placed so as to become the focus of adoration; in a typical Protestant church the pulpit localizes attention; while in a Friends Meetinghouse there is no visible point of concentration, worship being here directed neither toward the actions nor the words of others, but toward the inward experience of the gathered group.[1]

Theologian Veli-Matti Kärkkäinen places Quakers squarely in the camp of Free Church tradition, citing "unmediated access to God" as one of the basic tenets of that tradition. While this accounts for the strong sense of individualism prevalent among Friends, it also forms the basis of corporate Quaker worship wherein ministry is assumed to be an equal partnership involving all believers.[2] Whether they claim the pastoral or non-pastoral system, Friends see the worship event as that which connects people equally and directly with God.

While it is rare to find a meetinghouse for programmed Friends that doesn't look like a Protestant church inside, the focus of the meeting is still less on the words and actions of the pastor than on the recognition and celebration of the presence of Christ in the midst of the worshipers. This view of Christ's immediate presence has been with Friends since their earliest days, and it stems from the Society's emphasis on "realized eschatology," meaning that Christ's reign is present and active in the here and now and not merely as anticipated future event.

Realized eschatology forms the basis of Friends ecclesiology. It comes from Friends taking seriously the message of Christ in the gospels. Jesus said things like "the kingdom of heaven is at hand" (Matthew 3:2; 4:17), and, "the kingdom of God is within you" (Luke 17:21); and Friends believe it; and believing it, they want to put the principles and practices of God's reign into their lives and actions.

Realized eschatology has a profound effect on the way Friends view the church. It is not a people gathered in anticipation of the coming of Christ. Neither is it a people commemorating the work their Savior accomplished on a cross two millennia ago. When Friends gather for worship, no matter whether a pastor is present, they are gathering *with Christ* to worship God in spirit and in truth. It is this distinct interpretation of eschatology and its commensurate effect on ecclesiology that gives form to the Quaker experience. This form comes to life in the worship, administrative work, and witness of the meeting.

### The Presence in Worship

Friends place great weight on founder George Fox's statement that "the Lord Christ Jesus was come to teach his people himself."[3] That means Friends believe every worship experience is a divine encounter—Christ and we are there together. While most, if not all, Christians acknowledge Jesus' promise, "For where two or three are gathered in my name, I am there among them" (Matthew 18:20 NRSV), Friends base their worship on it. They expect Christ to meet with them and to speak to them whenever they gather for worship. This may sound both common *and* strange to Christians. It is as if—cognitively—many Christians assent to Christ's presence, but—behaviorally—act as if he were light years away. Listening for God in worship? That's weird. To this, Elton Trueblood replies, "Is there anything queer or strange in listening together for God's voice? What would be really *strange* would be a conversation in which one did all of the talking."[4]

As explained in the previous chapter, prior to the advent of the pastoral movement among Friends in the 1880s, virtually all Quaker meetings for worship were held on what has come to be known as "the basis of silence." Trueblood takes issue with this phrase, believing a more accurate description would be the suggestion of Thomas Kelly that Friends meet "on the basis of Holy Obedience," not determining to be silent or vocal, but to obediently respond to God's leading.[5] Many Friends today, particularly those in Europe and North America, continue this practice unaided by paid pastoral ministers.

Unprogrammed Friends—the ones without paid pastors—generally begin worship in silence, waiting for the Spirit to speak within and to reveal whether that which is spoken is intended for more than just the individual worshiper. That Friends take seriously God's place in this process is indicated by how few persons, in the normal course of a worship event, actually speak. The point is not to "share what's on one's heart" or deliver an interpretation of the Sunday news or preach a sermon—it is to speak forth the word of God. The speaker functions as "the immediate mouthpiece of the group of worshipers whose insight into Truth has been brought to utterance by the Holy Spirit, the Presence in the midst."[6] The diagram on the next page, by the late Quaker pastor Stan Thornburg, illustrates the process by which Friends discern the leading of the Spirit with respect to speaking in worship.[7]

Presence-driven worship is found not only among unprogrammed Friends; it is also foundational to worship among those Friends who have adopted the pastoral system. Most programmed Quaker meetings include some element of open or waiting worship in which the same process is followed. The difference is often in duration. In programmed worship, a pastor or worship leader, in conjunction with the Holy Spirit through prayer and deliberate meditation, chooses hymns and readings appropriate for worship. These are

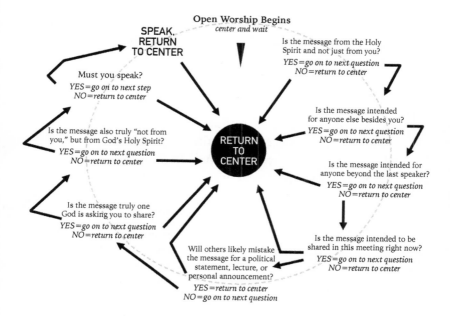

**Open Worship Begins**
*center and wait*

SPEAK,
RETURN
TO CENTER

**RETURN TO CENTER**

Must you speak?
*YES=go on to next step*
*NO=return to center*

Is the message also truly "not from you," but from God's Holy Spirit?
*YES=go on to next question*
*NO=return to center*

Is the message truly one God is asking you to share?
*YES=go on to next question*
*NO=return to center*

Will others likely mistake the message for a political statement, lecture, or personal announcement?
*YES=return to center*
*NO=go on to next question*

Is the message from the Holy Spirit and not just from you?
*YES=go on to next question*
*NO=return to center*

Is the message intended for anyone else besides you?
*YES=go on to next question*
*NO=return to center*

Is the message intended for anyone beyond the last speaker?
*YES=go on to next question*
*NO=return to center*

Is the message intended to be shared in this meeting right now?
*YES=go on to next question*
*NO=return to center*

often connected with a message or sermon prepared in advance by a pastor or elder under the guidance of the Spirit. Open worship, a time of silence out of which anyone who feels led by the Spirit can speak, will either precede or follow the sermon and/or other parts of the worship event. The duration of this worship can be from two or three minutes to fully half the meeting, depending on the leading of the Spirit or the preference of the meeting. In some cases, it may last even longer.

It is unlikely that Friends will ever agree on the place of paid pastors in the life of a meeting, or, even among those meetings with a pastoral staff and printed orders of worship, the proper location and duration of open worship. Yet when Friends come together, whether in a quiet meetinghouse in London or a contemporary worship center in La Paz, they do so in the expectation that God will meet with them and speak to them.

It is this expectancy that draws them to meeting week after week. It also guides them in the way they do the business of the church.

## The Presence in Business

Suppose for just a minute that you are chair of a church board charged with administration of a particular area of ministry. After pouring yourself a cup of coffee, you take your seat at the meeting table prepared to do business. Suddenly, the door to the boardroom opens and in walks Jesus Christ. He smiles, shakes a few hands, pours his cup of coffee, and takes a seat beside you. Would there be a difference in how church business is conducted at that meeting? Would majority rule? Would the meeting look any different than that of a corporate board of directors bounded beginning and end by brief prayers, or would there be constant interaction with the One for whom the church exists to adore?

For members of the Society of Friends, every meeting in which the business of the church is conducted is a meeting in which Jesus is present. This stems directly from Friends' belief in the immediate presence of Christ in worship. In fact, among many Friends, the business meeting is known by its full name: *meeting for worship with a concern for business.*

While church business meetings can have many purposes and may involve the entire membership of a congregation or just those serving on a committee or board, they all share one distinction: they are settings for the decision-making processes of the church. Because Friends expect the immediate presence of Christ in their business meetings, their method of coming to decisions is not based on choosing the best or most viable option but on discovering the will of God for the meeting or group. This process of discovery has been called consensus, but that may be misleading. Wilmer Cooper rejects this word, saying, "Consensus is at heart a secular approach that defies the very theological foundations of Quaker faith and practice." Cooper sees consensus as "attempts to accommodate conflicting wills and interests."[8] This purely human practice, even when performed in a church setting, may encourage people to listen better to each other and perhaps argue less enthusiastically, but it will not enable a group to discern the will of God.

Another misinterpretation of Quaker decision making is unanimity: that every member of the meeting or group must agree before a decision is made. Cooper asserts, "This assumes a political model requiring that every person (i.e., every 'vote') must be counted in the affirmative in order for the meeting to take action."[9] While full agreement may be a worthy outcome of the process, it once again focuses on the human, rather than the God-ward side of the equation. A decision made outside of God's will is wrong even if it is ratified by one hundred percent of the congregation.

How then do Friends conduct business when Christ is expected to be present in their meetings? First, as was previously mentioned, they begin with worship, the expectant waiting on the Presence in the midst. Of this part of the process, Lloyd Lee Wilson writes,

> This period of waiting worship which precedes meeting for business is a time of personal centering down into that Life which guides us, and a time of prayer for the faith community

which is about to seek to know and carry out the will of God. This opening worship should therefore never be allowed to become perfunctory, nor should it be hurried by the burden of difficult decisions ahead. On the contrary, it often seems that the meeting's ability to find unity in the Spirit is enhanced by a deeper opening worship, and more time spent in worship at the beginning of meeting for business means less is needed later on to reach unity on matters that had previously seemed quite difficult.[10]

After some time of waiting worship, as Friends sense the presence of Christ among them, they begin to take up the issues of business at hand. A clerk guides the process as he or she seeks a "sense of the meeting," what those present "discern to be the inward leading of the Spirit."[11] Jack Willcuts describes the scene as follows:

> It sometimes works this way: when Smith speaks following Jones, he takes into consideration Jones's opinion. Brown may follow with a statement that would probably have been different had Smith and Jones not spoken. Every member credits every other sincere member with at least some insight. Finally, a decision is made that receives the approval of all. A number of persons then say, "I approve," "I agree," or some equivalent expression. The result is more than mere group dynamics or courteous dialogue, although the Spirit may use both.

The ideal of all business decisions is to reach unified action as a sense of the Holy Spirit's leading. If this can be found without division and in a warmth of spiritual guidance, the ideal is realized.[12]

But what if things don't go so smoothly? As with any decision-making process, a number of roadblocks can appear. However, when the process is driven not by personal desires but by the Presence in the midst, these roadblocks are surmountable. One such case might involve a decision interpreted by the clerk to be the sense of the meeting that is not agreed upon by one or even a few of the members. Remembering that the goal of the process is discernment of God's will for the whole, and not the appeasement of every individual part, those persons may *stand aside*, publicly making it clear that they do not agree with the decision but nevertheless submit to the will of the meeting.

Of course, since Quaker meetings are made up of real people like you and me, things don't always go as smoothly as the ideal. There are times when someone disagrees and will not stand aside. It is then up to the clerk, guided by the Spirit, to discern what is right for the meeting as a whole, and based on that discernment, to allow the decision to go forward—or not.

Another roadblock to decision making may be the recognition that no discernment, no clear answer, has been given that would lead to an immediate decision. Most Friends would not consider this a roadblock, but rather an indication that the Spirit is at work and has instructed Friends to wait a while longer for a clear leading. Once again, it is Friends' foundation in the immediate presence of Christ in their midst, and the expectation of his speaking to them, that drives the process, even when the process takes a while—sometimes an uncomfortably long while—to reach completion. Friends' decisions concerning slavery exemplify the lengthy period of waiting sometimes involved.

Quakers, now known for their stringent anti-slavery stance, spent decades laboring over the issue. Even so, ridding the Society of slaveholders, speaking out against slavery, and ultimately becoming a strong voice for abolition was a process, and yearly meetings across America found no clarity until years of discernment produced the anti-slavery decisions with which Friends are identified.

Friends historian Thomas Hamm dates the start of American Friends' opposition to slavery to a "protest," or petition, sent from Quakers in Germantown, Pennsylvania, to Philadelphia Yearly Meeting in 1688.[13] That petition was tabled by the yearly meeting after significant deliberation. It was not brought up again until 1696, when petitions by William Southeby and other Friends reached the yearly meeting floor. At that meeting an "advice" was written that urged, "Friends be careful not to encourage the bringing in of any more Negroes."[14] Philadelphia Yearly Meeting did not take further action regarding the slave trade until Ralph Sandiford published the vehemently antislavery pamphlet, *A Brief Examination of the Practice of the Times*, in 1729. The yearly meeting's action was to disown Friend Sandiford.[15] Finally in 1776, in response to efforts by Friends like John Woolman and Anthony Benezet, Philadelphia Yearly Meeting "became the first major religious body to require its members to cease and desist from slaveholding."[16]

The lengthy process by which Philadelphia Friends became the anti-slavery institution for which they are known was repeated in yearly meetings across the United States, with some yearly meetings, such as Indiana, splitting over the issue.[17] Why did it take so long for Friends to reach unity on a decision that now seems obvious? Perhaps they were waiting to hear God's voice clearly among the many voices declaring—often quite loudly—their personal, religious, and political views. Friends believe God is there in every monthly or yearly meeting session, but distinguishing God's voice takes a high degree of humility on the part of all Friends involved, along with strong leadership, skilled at the art of interpreting the sense of the meeting.

Because they are constantly seeking that sense of the meeting in which God's will is known and God's presence felt, Friends are generally not surprised when God shows up at a meeting for worship or speaks up at a meeting for business. It is just such an expectation that propels these two aspects of their ecclesiology. It also drives the third essential part of their view of the church—its witness in the world.

## The Presence in the World

Before anyone can understand how Friends look at the mission of the church, they must recognize a fundamental doctrine of Quakerism that rises from the basic premise of the immediate presence of God; namely, that this presence is not confined to working solely within believers. Early Quaker apologist Robert Barclay referred to the light and the seed that come from God and are present in every person, guiding them toward their Source:

When we speak of the seed or light we understand a spiritual, celestial, and invisible principle, a principle in which God dwells as Father, Son, and Spirit. A measure of this divine and glorious principle exists as a seed in all men which by its nature draws, invites, and inclines the individual toward God. Some call this the *vehiculum Dei*, or the spiritual body of Christ, the flesh and blood of Christ, which came down from heaven, and on which all who have faith are fed and nourished with eternal life. The light and seed witnesses against and reproves every unrighteous action.[18]

For Barclay and for most Friends today, this means that in some sense the real presence of Christ is present in all humankind, even prior to any conscious claiming of salvation. The mission of the church, then, is not to find ways of getting God into people but of drawing out or actuating the seed that is already there. George Fox described the task of early Friends as walking "cheerfully over the world, answering that of God in every one."[19] Once again, it comes to that Divine Presence, active in the world, moving Friends' religious experience.

A classic story of one Friend, Mary Fisher, visiting the Sultan of Turkey, shows an evangelist seeking not to convert a lost soul but to help a person move closer to the God of whom he already had some knowledge. Fisher made the trip to Adrianople (present day Edirne) to bring Sultan Mahomet IV a message she claimed was from the Lord. The sultan received her words graciously, then inquired as to her knowledge of Mohammad. Howard Brinton recounts, "She replied 'that she knew him not, but Christ enlightened every man who came into the world. Him she knew... And concerning [Mohammad] she said, 'they might judge him false or true according to the words and prophecies he spoke.' The Turk confessed this to be true."[20]

How then do Friends take this sense of mission into their world? While it is tempting to divide Quaker mission into the traditional areas of evangelism and social action, Friends have never separated the two. According to Wilmer Cooper, "Friends believe the Gospel is both personal and social and therefore must be concerned with the whole person and the whole world."[21] Early Friends were a missionary movement with "a fervent zeal to spread the Truth in spite of violent and cruel opposition by both Church and State."[22] That zeal for the Gospel, coupled with the recognition of the seed of God in everyone, propelled them quickly into the political arena where they championed the cause of the disenfranchised and marginalized. Friends were at the forefront of the anti-slavery movement, prison reform, public education, labor reform, and care for the mentally ill. Today, Quaker organizations such as the Friends Committee for National Legislation, American Friends Service Committee, and Right Sharing of World Resources work hard to bring about significant social change, all because they sense that this Presence which is active in their meeting for worship, is within all persons regardless of racial, cultural, or economic background. Any meeting with another person, then, is an opportunity to bear witness to the presence of God at that place and in that moment. The result may be a political action or a spiritual revival, but the impetus is the same Presence in the midst.

It is my conviction, as I hope these pages have shown, that Friends' perception of church, which I have called ecclesiology, is at the core of how they live in the world. For Friends, God is actively engaged in the world and in the church, co-participating with them in worship, business, and mission. But what does that look like in the everyday activities of ministry? How does God show up in a church service? Where does Jesus sit at the meeting of the religious education committee? How do we respond to that of God in others? And what is the pastor's place in all this? The remaining chapters of this book are devoted to providing some answers to those questions, beginning with a look at the Quaker pastor's role in the worship service.

# ▪ 3 ▪

## Pin-Drop Moments:
## The Friends Pastor and Worship

I am a creature of habit, a trait I inherited from my father and grandfather, and dutifully passed to my son. I do things the same way every time: no exceptions. Breaks in routine drive me crazy. So in the fall of 2005, when I obtained my first cell phone, I began a Sunday ritual that continued throughout my tenure as pastor at Williamsburg Friends. Each week I would enter the worship room twenty minutes or so before Sunday school, remove from my pockets my phone and car keys, turn off the phone, and place those items on the pew that sits out of sight behind the organ. One Sunday in 2009, I did not. I don't know why. I just forgot to turn off my phone and put it on the pew. It should not have been a big deal since I never get phone calls on Sunday morning anyway. All my contacts know I'm a pastor and generally busy at 10:35 a.m. on a Sunday morning. I didn't even notice the phone still in my pocket until it rang the moment I stood to read the call to worship, a verse from the Psalms.

It wasn't the obnoxious ring of an incoming call, just the gentle jingle of a text message, with accompanying vibration. But it was loud enough, with me standing in front of our spectacularly sensitive lectern microphone, to be heard throughout the meetinghouse.

I was embarrassed. Such a thing had never happened to me before. My first inclination was to ignore it and maybe turn the phone off during a hymn or something. My second inclination was to give the congregation a sheepish look, remove the offending appliance from my pocket, and turn it off while apologizing profusely to everyone. Then a thought quietly formed in my heart. What if it was God texting?

Before you think I am totally off my rocker, let me explain. Remember I said I always removed my keys and phone from my pockets and set them on the hidden pew? Remember I said I was a creature of habit? When I always do something, I *always* do something. No exceptions. Because I am so predictable, I had to wonder, "Why did I not turn my phone off and put it on the pew?" This really bothered me. I always did that. Always. Why not today? Was there more to this than simple forgetfulness? The conversation in my head took place over a period of about two seconds. I doubt any of the people at worship knew what was happening.

What I did next might be called Quaker instinct. I told the meeting, "I just received a text message. You know how I always turn my phone off when I'm here; well today I forgot. And I *never* forget. So I'm going to go ahead and check my phone. What the heck? I'll read the message out loud. Maybe it's something for all of us." I opened the phone and read these words from a songwriter friend in Toronto:

> Let all the people of the world pray for everyone else but themselves. I always find it brings pure peace for those few moments.

You could have heard the proverbial pin drop. The worshipers and I knew something had happened, although one might have been hard-pressed to put a label on it. I said, "I believe we've heard our call to worship. In light of it, let's take some time for silent prayer, remembering others in our community and our world."

Pin-drop moments. I guess that describes what Quaker pastors routinely expect in meetings for worship. We come to meeting knowing that what we or our worship teams have diligently and meticulously planned for the day may not happen—and that's okay. Our plans are not always God's plans, even if they seemed like it when we made them. It is perfectly fine with us if God changes them. When God does, if we are expecting that change and willing to let it happen, then pin-drop moments occur; and our breath, as well as our words, are taken away.

Sometimes pin-drop moments disrupt or absolutely destroy the order of worship. One Sunday morning in 2003, a young man named Aaron (I change the names of some individuals whose stories I tell, but I always try to keep the essence of the story as true as possible) picked up two older men, Earl and William, both with some form of intellectual disability, and brought them to the Williamsburg Meeting, as he had been doing every week for a year. On this particular morning, Aaron shared some exciting news on the way to worship. Mike, the man who had first introduced these men to Quaker worship, had suffered a heart attack during a train trip in his native Germany. Aaron related the story of how Mike had stood up in the train, felt a sharp pain in his left arm, and passed out. Fortunately, near Mike on the train was a physician who immediately rendered aid and may have saved Mike's life. Aaron, Earl, and William talked about the incident, and how Mike had recovered, as they continued the drive to Williamsburg.

Worship began as usual at Williamsburg Friends that Sunday. I gave the announcements, people stood and greeted one another, and Bill, the song leader, led the first hymn. There were a few moments for centering down before the morning's message. All of a sudden, from the silence came Earl's voice. Earl was an enthusiastic singer who knew all the old hymns and sang them loudly, although his timing was always a beat or two off. However, Earl could barely speak a complete sentence, and those he did speak came out as jumbled words and guttural sounds.

On this morning, Earl tried to speak words. He blurted something out, but I couldn't understand him. Besides, it wasn't yet time for open worship. That was supposed to come later, after the sermon and more singing. Earl kept talking, repeating his gibberish. Aaron listened intently but could not make out the words or their intention. Then Earl began crying, his tears pleading for someone to understand. On previous occasions, when Earl wanted to say something, William could sometimes interpret, but on this day, William was sound asleep in a rocking chair in the back of the worship room. I came down from the pulpit, got on my knees before Earl, held his hands and tried to console him, but he would not be consoled, and his frustration grew.

At this point, I was beginning to suspect that Earl had a true message from God to deliver to the meeting. I also knew no one in the meeting at that moment could figure out what the message was. Going out on a hermeneutical limb, I referred to what I thought might be a biblical precedent and said, "In First Corinthians 12, Paul wrote about spiritual gifts in the church. He said there was a gift of speaking in tongues, speaking in a language not known to the speaker. Paul also mentioned the gift of interpretation, given so others in the church could understand the messages given in tongues so everyone could benefit from the message. Friends, Earl has given us a message, but we can't understand it. I believe God has placed within our congregation today someone who will be able to interpret Earl's message. And we can't go on until we hear that interpretation. So even though it's not time for open worship, we're going to go into a time of silence. And we're going to stay there until God raises up an interpreter."

The Williamsburg meetinghouse grew silent for a few minutes, five, maybe seven. An air of expectancy filled the room. Then Aaron spoke directly to Earl. "Earl," he said, "Are you saying, 'Tell them about his arm?'"

Earl started shaking his head up and down vigorously. As distraught as he seemed earlier from frustration, he now was beside himself with joy. Then Aaron related to the meeting the story of Mike's train ride, the pain in his arm, his heart attack, and the lifesaving treatment by the doctor who just happened to be there.

Earl's joy spread throughout the congregation. They felt as if they'd been directly in the presence of God. Rather than try to turn the service back in the direction I'd originally planned, I attempted to summarize what had just happened, allowing others to add their perceptions. Then it was time for singing, the offering, and a little more open worship—the scheduled kind. That day you might not have heard a pin drop—the joyful noise was overwhelming—but I'm sure that pin dropped all the same.

Somewhere in the files of my laptop sits the bulletin for that Sunday. It lists an order of worship, the sermon text and title, and a few hymns I thought might support the sermon. But other than the first few items, none of that happened, at least not in my desired order. In a Friends meeting, that's perfectly all right. And that's one of the things that make the worship experience different for the Quaker pastor.

A Friends pastor I met while researching these differences said, about how Quaker pastors, and Friends in general, perceive worship, "For Friends, every meeting for worship is an adventure. Even when programming is planned, there needs to be a constant sensitivity to the Spirit that frees us to joyfully discard or rearrange the planned programming."*

I truly believe most seminary graduates see the worship service as an adventure. I think they want something exciting to happen. They want to know the Spirit of God is present with their congregation on Sunday morning. But something happens between the anticipation and the pulpit. Dozens, or maybe hundreds, of years of tradition beg to be included in the plan. Then the anticipation turns into a litany of what-has-always-been and the sense of adventure slowly gets pushed out of the way.

The Friends pastor lives for the adventure. We don't see worship as a totally planned experience. The sense of spontaneity that was the core of seventeenth century Quaker experience still permeates twenty-first

---

*Throughout this book I will refer to stories, opinions, and statements shared with me by numerous Friends pastors and a variety of other religious leaders. These were all shared during research I conducted over a number of years via surveys and phone, email, and in-person conversations. I recorded this input for myself, but it is not available in any reference I can cite. I have only used their names when they have given me specific permission to do so.

century pastoral meetings, in spite of worship bulletins that show an order of worship. Occasionally, over a period of weeks or months, the meeting for worship at 'Old First Friends Church' might get a bit inflexible and orderly, but then someone will play the Tom Hanks character from *A League of Their Own* and remind us, "There is no order in worship!"

Of course, few pastoral Friends meetings function well without that worship bulletin. I've always used one. At Williamsburg Friends, where I pastored from 1999-2015, we liked to think of the printed order of worship as a suggestion rather than an order. Sometimes we followed the plan to the letter, and sometimes right from the start things went merrily off on the winds of the Spirit.

While it may seem all right for the Spirit to mess with our order of worship, one of the things we pastors tend to like to keep for ourselves is public prayer. Growing up, I seldom heard anyone but my pastor pray during the worship service. I think he felt that public prayer was his duty as pastor, but also his privilege, and he took it very seriously. It is difficult for some pastors to entrust to just anyone the holy act of praying aloud before the church. Even when we'd like to include more public pray-ers, volunteers don't line up to take advantage of the opportunity. So it's easier just to do it ourselves. At least we know it will be done well. And then, sometimes, another pin drops.

One September morning I got a phone call from a former student, Carl, who was pastoring a Friends meeting in another state. He was experiencing some difficulties in the meeting and needed some support. He said he was coming to Earlham School of Religion's annual Pastors Conference the following weekend. I invited him to worship at Williamsburg, where he'd been an intern, and told him the folks there would pray for him.

On the Sunday before the conference, Carl arrived at meeting for worship. During the meeting, I told the folks Carl was going through a rough time and asked the members of Ministry and Oversight (if you don't speak Quakerese, M&O committees are like elders) to come forward and lay their hands on Carl for prayer. As they were coming forward and Carl was standing at the front of the worship room, William spoke up, "Can I pray too?"

William, as you may recall, was the occasional translator for Earl. He liked to sleep in the rocking chair at the back of the meeting room. William was very vocal, often making a comment or asking a question in the middle of my sermon. Occasionally, his interjections were on topic. Mostly, they could be summed up in his most famous statement, given with all due pomp as he stood before the assembled meeting, "I gotta go poop!"

Expecting a word of poop, but not wishing to quench William's spirit—I didn't really give a thought to any other Spirit that might be in operation at that moment—I invited him to come forward with the M&O members. No sooner had William placed his hand on Carl's head than he began to speak. For the next half-minute or so, William prayed the most eloquent and appropriate prayer anyone could have prayed under the same circumstances. He ended with an amen, and the meetinghouse was engulfed in holy silence. Another pin-drop moment as we all recognized that Jesus had just prayed aloud for Carl.

Of course, being wide open to the Spirit's leading leaves one vulnerable to the occasional misread. Maybe this is why we struggle so hard with letting go of our control of the worship service.

I remember a Sunday morning when Ralph stood up to pray in meeting. Ralph was a personal friend, fellow singer/songwriter, and occasional churchgoer. He sometimes sang one of his songs during worship. I'm not sure how appropriate pirate shanties are as an offertory, but that may be a matter of interpretation. Anyway, Ralph began praying a fine, very "pastoral" kind of prayer. I was impressed with my liturgical leadership in giving him the space to pray. Then, subtly at first, Ralph's prayer changed. Soon it was a paean to Ralph himself. After a minute or so of this self-lovefest, I said something I've never said in church before and don't ever expect to again—"Shut up, Ralph." I didn't say it in anger, and I didn't say it with a verbal exclamation point. I just said it clearly and convincingly.

You could have heard a pin drop that day too, but not with joy. Ralph and I had a little chat after worship where I explained my response to his "prayer." He sulked for a couple of weeks and then returned to meeting with his guitar and pirate songs. I guess, at least in my ecclesiology, there is room in church for pirates but not for braggarts. Members of Ministry and Oversight agreed with my response to Ralph, even the words I used. Sometimes, you leave room for the Spirit, but you only get Ralph. No one ever said being a Quaker pastor was easy.

In spite of our hesitancy to be vulnerable in worship, pin-drop moments happen again and again in Friends meetings for worship. They happen in other congregations as well. I've heard pastors from other denominations tell about them. But they happen almost accidentally outside of Quaker meetings (and sometimes *in* Quaker meetings). Too often the door that could lead to their happening is not opened far enough by the one called to give spiritual leadership to the congregation. I've heard pastors say, "I wish I could do that in my church." I want to tell them they can, but I know that in many cases, liturgical practices or church polity won't let them.

So how can we make room for pin-drop moments? It's a tough question. It's like asking how to catch a breeze. Yet, in regard to worship, our responsibility as Friends pastors is to create a space for just that miracle to happen. Over the years I've developed a simple formula that comes with no guarantees but might help us make that catch.

First, there's expectation. We need to expect God's intervention in our meetings. Pin-drop moments, I believe, are on the verge of happening anytime. That's because God is always there. Remember the *Presence in the Midst* painting? It's true. If we know God is meeting with us, then we can reasonably and excitedly expect God to take an active part in worship. True, it doesn't always happen. I don't know why. Does God have nothing to say? Are we not in the proper frame of mind to hear God? I don't know. I do know, however, that we will rarely experience God's active presence in meeting unless we expect it.

The second part of the formula is observation. We need to see God in those little things that happen in worship, things we often take for granted.

Do you remember that part in *The Matrix* where Neo sees a cat cross a doorway and then sees the same cat cross the same doorway a few seconds later? It's a glitch in the Matrix, an indication that something is not quite right, the evidence that he is living in a world that is not all it seems to be. We, not just Quaker pastors but all of us, live in a world like that, and the glitches are often glimpses into a reality where the Spirit is moving all the time.

Perhaps the question we need to be asking is, What if? What if the thing you are seeing differently today is trying to tell you something? What if that inconvenience is an act of God? What if the little thing you forgot to do for the first time in your life is an open door to the Spirit? Sometimes there really are two cats and no message to be heard. But sometimes, maybe more often than we think, there's a glitch in the Matrix, and if we're looking carefully we can see God at work.

The last part of the formula is assumption. If we expect God to be present and we are observing those little glitches in our routine, then for us to experience the pin-drop moment we have to assume it is God who is breaking in.

This can be tricky. Many of us tend to analyze the glitches rather than act on them. We ask the what-if questions, but then we list in our minds all the impossibilities. I think for us to increase the frequency of our pin-drop moments we need to go out on a proverbial limb. Given the choice of whether something might be God or whether it might be last night's porridge, let's assume it's God. We will be wrong sometimes, and that could get embarrassing. Imagine the look on my face if that text from God had turned out to be a "How the f*** are you?" message from an old college chum. But we will be right about it enough to enjoy that *Presence in the Midst* a lot more often and to help our congregations/ meetings do so as well.

The planning and order of service is not the only place where Friends expect Christ to show up, often unexpectedly, and often through laypersons (a term of distinction Friends generally avoid). Even in the sermon, the part of the worship many think belongs to the pastor, Friends know God sometimes makes an appearance in unexpected ways and through unexpected people.

# ■ 4 ■

## Handing Out the Keys:
## The Friends Pastor and Preaching

*A*t a Friends pastors retreat some time ago, the speaker, who was not a Quaker, gave a personal illustration of how the sermon functions in the life of a congregation. He told of a time when he had the rare opportunity to meet with evangelist Billy Graham at Billy's home in North Carolina. Mr. Graham lived at the top of a mountain. His property was surrounded by a fence, and there was a security gate that visitors would stop at before they could have access to the residential area.

The speaker went on to describe how he and some friends drove up to the Graham compound security gate, where he showed his invitation to visit Billy. Since the invitation was for him alone, the speaker left his friends outside the gate and, when it opened, he walked the rest of the way up the mountain to the Graham house. While there, the speaker had a wonderful conversation with Mr. Graham about things of the Spirit. When the visit was over, the speaker walked back down the mountain, anxious to tell his friends waiting outside the gate about that conversation. He concluded that the work of the pastor was to spend time on the mountain with God during the week and then bring God's words to the people waiting below.

The farther along the speaker went in his story, the more tension built up in the banquet hall where the meeting was taking place. As one of the attendees, I sensed something not quite right about what the speaker was saying, and I was glad others were sensing it too. It meant I might not have to be the one to shoot my mouth off. And I wasn't. No sooner had the speaker finished this illustration of which he seemed quite proud than one of the Quaker pastors seated in the audience rose to speak.

"Excuse me," he said, "We don't see it that way."

This took the speaker aback, but he graciously asked the pastor to explain what he meant. The pastor smiled and answered, "Well, as Quakers, I guess we agree that it's important for the pastor to spend time with God during the week. And it is kind of like going up a mountain. The thing is, when we come back to our people, we don't just bring them a word from God, we unlock the gate and hand out the keys."

The number of heads nodding in agreement gave a strong indication of the Quaker view of the sermon and the creative process that accompanies it. Because we believe that Christ the Teacher has come to all of us directly, Friends pastors don't claim to have a corner on truth. Although we diligently prepare our sermons, we know the greater goal is to help our congregants listen to that Teacher and receive the message themselves. When it works, it can make for an exciting, but sometimes disturbing, preaching event.

To describe that event, perhaps first I should explain a bit about how Friends pastors view the sermon and sermon preparation. Then I will go on to share some stories about what happens when sermon preparation meets the immediate sense of the Teacher's presence.

One North Carolina Friends pastor says, "Sermons should be seen as 'prep' work for real worship which comes in the time of quiet waiting." To understand that statement, we need to look at the fundamental difference between the way Reformation churches view the sermon as opposed to pre-Reformation churches.

The Church, with a very large capital "C," that massive institution in existence long before Martin Luther, focused its worship on sacrament, participation in the body and blood of Christ. Sermons were secondary to the act of Holy Communion. The churches that came out of the Reformation, with their high view of scripture, moved the sacrament to a place secondary to preaching. Although communion is still of vital importance in many Protestant denominations, the sermon is the high point to which worship services ascend.

It's different with Friends. We see that time of communion with God, what many Friends would call waiting worship or open worship, as the high point of the service. The greatest feeling Friends can get, in my opinion, is that of being in what Quakers call a "gathered" meeting. That is when everyone present knows they are in the presence of God. It's a kind of holy hush. At best, a sermon might help us move toward that point. So the idea of a sermon being prep work for worship makes sense among Friends.

Along with the goal of a gathered worship experience, Friends pastors bring with them into their study (or coffee shop or park bench or pub) a sense that the Spirit who inspired the scripture text is still speaking today. For Quakers, the Bible is not a closed book, physically or metaphorically. When we read the Bible, we engage with texts written at points in time to specific audiences. We value the various kinds of literary and historical criticism that help us understand those times and audiences. At the same time, we believe the Spirit can use those ancient passages to speak to us today. The Spirit may even use the text as a jumping off point for a new (as if there really were anything new under the sun) word from God.

Perhaps another Friends United Meeting* pastor said it best,

> A sermon needs to grow out of the pastor's interaction with the Holy Spirit, the Spirit's expression in the meeting and the others in the meeting, in the same way [those] expressions in unprogrammed worship are to rise out of the Spirit's presence in the attenders at meeting. "Church calendars" are secondary. A pastor may prepare a sermon but should not be surprised if the Spirit brings a different message.

I like the way that pastor looked at messages from both the programmed (pastoral) and unprogrammed point of view. One of the age-old criticisms of prepared preaching among Friends is that advance preparation must be the enemy of Spirit leadership. How can you listen for the Spirit's message in worship if you have already prepared a message to speak? Good question, to which I and other Friends pastors would answer, by listening to that Spirit through the sermon development process and continuing to listen even when you think

---

*The pastors I quote in this book represent two of the main bodies of Quakers in the world: Friends United Meeting (FUM) and Evangelical Friends Church (EFC). Most meetings/churches that are members of these bodies are pastoral, or programmed; that is, they offer compensation to individuals engaged in pastoral ministry.

the sermon is finished. Your sermon very well might be finished. However, as a Quaker pastor, you know that sermon you prepared may not be the message God will give your meeting on Sunday.

If you are a Quaker pastor, then you probably understand this paradox. If not, perhaps a few examples will help your understanding. Let's start with the times when the Spirit changes the message and move to the times when the Spirit changes the messenger.

Quaker educator and pastor Catherine Griffith recalls times when she knew her prepared message was not the one God planned for her meeting on a given Sunday. Although it has not happened often in her experience, she describes those times as "having that feeling and knowing that I would need to tell the congregation that the morning wasn't going to go the way they expected." Griffith relates in detail one of those occasions,

> I think I hoped that some miracle would happen, and a message would arrive at the last minute, delivering me from the need to say, "I have no message to bring to you this morning."

> As was my habit, before the pastoral prayer I asked if people had anything they wanted to bring before God that morning. One person shared a deep concern, then another and another. The pauses after each one deepened with prayerful caring. One man spoke up, "Catherine, I don't think you're supposed to preach today."

> "That's good," I replied. "God didn't give me a message to bring." Laughter, relief, awe.

It was a deeply blessed Sunday, sharing and caring and praying for one another. And one more reminder that trusting the still, small voice is always a good idea.

For some reason, which I am glad not to know, God has a habit of changing Easter messages on me. Every year, the Williamsburg meeting where I pastored and the local Nazarene church hold a joint Easter celebration. It used to be a sunrise service, but it keeps moving later in the morning. Last time I was there it was held at 8:00 a.m. On alternate years, one church hosts the service and cooks the breakfast while the other church provides the speaker and any special music.

One Easter Sunday, I entered the Nazarene church fully prepared with a sermon. It was a more or less typical Easter sermon, but I thought it to be adequate. I had handwritten it on legal paper that was tucked into my Bible at the point of the text. The service moved along nicely with good music and joyous congregational singing. During the last hymn before the message, a little voice spoke to me, "Leave your message on your seat." All right, it wasn't, "If you build it, he will come," but it was just as clear. What wasn't clear was what would happen when I stepped behind the lectern.

The hymn ended, and the Nazarene pastor introduced me. I stood in the pulpit and asked the congregation of Friends and Nazarenes to enter into a brief time of silent waiting. They were silent. I was waiting for something to enter my mind—anything to fill the void. My sermon sat unopened on the chair upstage.

After a few moments, I started speaking. I must have quoted scripture because I heard some "Amens" from the Nazarenes. To this day I cannot recall a word I said in that sermon. However, whenever I run into a certain Nazarene family, be it at the supermarket or at another Easter service, I hear the words, "I'll never forget that message you preached on Easter the other year. It really spoke to me." I smile and tell them I appreciate hearing that, which I do. But I've never had the courage to ask what it was I said. Best not to know. The message was from God to them. I was the channel through which it flowed, and nothing more.

That's the way it is for the Friends preacher. We need to be able to exegete scripture and develop an interesting, motivating, and sometimes even fun sermon. We must be attuned to our listeners and prepare words both caring and prophetic. But we know that the Spirit who inspired those words in us during the week may have entirely different words for the rest of our meeting on Sunday. Funny thing is, whenever I've had a message preempted by the Spirit, I've never felt a need to preach the original message at a later date. It's like the message was fine for me that week, in that moment of time, but it never was meant for the church.

I've heard similar stories from pastors of various denominations. Most preachers know when a sermon they've prepared isn't quite right for the day or the audience assembled. I've known Baptists and Methodists, among others, who made the gutsy move of following a leading not to preach what they brought with them. It's not strictly a Quaker thing. But it does take sensitivity to the day-to-day movement of the Spirit and a willingness to set aside our plans for God's.

Then there are the times when God not only changes the message, God changes the messenger. This may be a truly Quaker phenomenon, because we're the ones with planned times of open worship. When we place that open worship time in front of the sermon, we risk the message of the day coming from someone other than ourselves. Still, in many Quaker meetings, we take that risk, although in just as many meetings we take the safer route and place open worship after the sermon as more of a reflective time based on the message. Sometimes the message and the messenger can't wait that long, which reminds me of Bart.

"Bart" was not his real name, but if you know the name Bart Simpson then you can imagine what this boy was like at age ten. He was not the pride and joy of the Northeastern School District, and when he attended meeting many Friends kept a suspicious eye on him. One Sunday, just before worship, Bart asked if he could say a few words during the service. Multiple scenarios flashed through my mind, none of them good, as I considered what it would mean to allow Bart access to the pulpit and a microphone. But I was a Friends pastor, and this was a meeting under the direction of the Spirit, not me. I told Bart to sit in the first row (he usually did anyway, the perfect place for heckling) and I would call on him during the meeting.

After the usual announcements, greetings, call to worship, and hymns, I told the congregation that Bart had asked to speak. Looks of horror passed across some of their faces. Bart stepped up to the lectern and told the meeting how the lesson he had heard in Sunday school had touched his life. He spoke for about two minutes to a hushed audience. When he was finished, I said, "I think we've heard God's message for today." We then entered a time of silence and open worship during which a couple of people verbally processed Bart's message. We all knew God was with us that day.

That was an example of the Spirit speaking through someone else on a Sunday morning. While guest speakers are not uncommon in any church or denomination, it is hard to imagine Bart being handed the preaching responsibility at 'Old First Church.' The expectation that the message of the morning could come from anywhere and anyone is something generally unique to Quaker pastors and the meetings that support them.

Henri Nouwen described his experience with God choosing the speaker in his book *In the Name of Jesus,* a book I've used in my class for Quaker pastors. I think the attitude Nouwen expresses is very much the attitude of the Quaker pastor.

In the Epilogue of *In the Name of Jesus,* Nouwen tells about a time he was invited to speak on Christian leadership at an event in Washington, D.C. He brought with him Bill, someone he worked with in Toronto at the L'Arche community for persons with intellectual disabilities. After Nouwen spoke, Bill asked if he might say something. This would have been highly irregular and was even more disconcerting because Nouwen would have no control over what Bill might say. Quaker preachers know exactly how this Catholic priest was feeling at that moment. Nouwen became a wonderful example for Friends when he gave Bill the microphone and listened as Bill added just the right words to Nouwen's original message.[1]

Of course, when pastors act on their belief that God's message can come from anyone at any time, they open the meeting to the potential of chaos if the Spirit is not truly in control. Kenyan Friend Simon Bulimo recently shared with me a situation in which some well-meaning folks commandeered the church for what proved to be less-than-Spirit–led purposes.

As he approached his church one Sunday, a few members met Bulimo outside and warned him there was some disruptive behavior taking place inside. When he entered the meetinghouse, he saw a small group of young persons moving through the assembled worshipers rebuking them for their sins and commanding them to leave the church. What intrigued Pastor Bulimo was the young people's ability to sense events happening in the worshipers' lives. He sat down to listen to the messages and pray for discernment as to their origin and intent.

Bulimo recalled taking some time to listen deeply to what the "prophets" were saying. He knew some in the congregation wanted him to put an immediate stop to the confusion, and yet he wanted to make sure he would not be quenching any work the Spirit might be doing in the lives of his meeting.

Finally, after what must have seemed to some congregants as too long a time, Bulimo heard a voice inside him saying it was time to call a halt to the rebuking. He stood among the people, prayed aloud, and then he told the speakers that all prophecy is subject to the Word of God, and the truth of their words must be discerned in light of scripture. He then led the meeting in singing. According to Bulimo, the group of young people turned their rebukes toward him and then marched out of the meetinghouse.

Simon Bulimo told me that story as a reminder that pastors need to be in constant discernment about when and from whom God's message may come, and about when a message may not be from God at all. I wish he had given specific instructions about how to tell the difference. Then again, maybe he did. Bulimo chose first the most Quakerly of all actions: he waited quietly. In spite of meeting members' discomfort—and who wouldn't be uncomfortable when being rebuked—this wise pastor waited, trusting that in time God would reveal the next step. No one ever said the pastor's job is easy, especially when we are trying to give as much space as possible for God to speak to and through God's people.

Friends never know for sure when or from whom God's words will spring. This could be quite problematic for the preacher expected to deliver a sermon roughly forty-eight weeks out of the year. How does one prepare a sermon she knows full well she may not present? That is the big question for those of us who are the paid preachers at any of the thousands of programmed meetings around the world. I have some ideas based on my own experience. They are not the be-all-and-end-all of homiletic theory, but they reflect my ideas as a preacher who listens to the Spirit as well as the text.

First of all, if we are going to preach the Bible, we need to give an adequate amount of time to exegeting the passages we preach. There's no getting around that. The Bible is far too often used as a weapon for attacking someone else's beliefs or as a strongbox for guarding our own. The common word for making the Bible say what we want it to say is *eisegesis*: reading into a text what we already believe. There is no room for the Spirit when sermons are planned based on such a process.

Exegesis, on the other hand, is a process of drawing out of the text what is actually in there. Of course, as my colleague Nancy Bowen reminds her students, "Interpretation matters and context is everything." Unless we expect the Spirit to reveal something completely new and outside the scriptures, we need to spend time getting our best understanding of the texts, their contexts, and the various ways they might be interpreted. Then, when we hear that "still small voice," we can be reasonably sure it is not our own.

There is no shortcut for good exegetical work, but exegesis does not a sermon make. If we really believe the Teacher is active today, then we need to make space for listening. I am a firm believer in starting sermon preparation early in the week. I try to read the text a few times on Monday or Tuesday, looking for areas that need deeper exegesis. Once I've done my digging, I leave the window seat at the donut shop or the college library, and I take to the golf course or the nursing home or the city park. In other words, I find a place to meditate on the text. I love to bounce ideas around in my head. Sometimes I meet with another pastor or two to get their input. Mostly I just listen for what the Spirit might be saying to me and to my congregation. This is one of the places where I believe the Present Teacher teaches, even though it is in advance of the meeting for worship.

Exegesis and meditation form the basis of most preachers' sermon preparation. What's the Quaker difference? I think we add one more part to the mix: expectation. More than any other group of pastors, Quakers fully expect the Holy Spirit to jump into the process. They expect that what happens on Sunday will be wonderful, possibly *un*expected, maybe even outlandish—a total departure from anything they imagined while they were studying. James wrote, "You have not because you ask not" (James 4:2). I think if we experience not, it is because we expect not. It's not really about us, our exegesis, our preparation, or even about our relationship with our meetings. For the

Friends pastor, it's about how week after week, we are always expecting a fresh breeze from God to blow us out of our socks. Sometimes that breeze flows through us, and sometimes it flows around us or through someone else.

# ▪ 5 ▪

## Walking Cheerfully:
## The Friends Pastor and Evangelism

Many years ago, I read an article in a weekly newspaper describing an upcoming missions conference held jointly by a Bible college and a nearby church. It featured the theme, "We Have It; They Don't." I guess the idea was that "it" was lacking in anyone but the conference planners and attenders. If "they" were ever to get "it," then "we" have to put it into them. That seems to be a pretty accurate description of evangelism in the mind of many Christians: filling the proverbial "God-shaped hole" everyone is alleged to have.

Friends, and their pastors, hold a different view of evangelism. It comes from advice George Fox gave to his followers to "walk cheerfully over the world, answering that of God in every one."[1] Although not all Friends agree on the specifics of how to follow Fox's instruction, most believe that God is already at work in the people they meet, be they Christians or adherents of any other religion or no religion. When I surveyed Friends pastors, educators, and superintendents* about this, one Evangelical Friends

---

*Friends decision-making bodies are geographically based, while being named by how often they gather for meeting for business. Generally the smallest bodies are the local church, or monthly meeting, which meet to make decisions together once each month. The highest decision-making body is the yearly meeting, which could cover part of one state, several states, or an entire country. There is no national or international decision-making body among Friends. A superintendent, or general or yearly meeting secretary, is the chief executive staff member of the yearly meeting.

pastor summed it up saying, "Quakerism does not attempt to introduce the unbeliever to God but to bring the unbeliever to recognition of the work of the Holy Spirit already calling and working in their lives."

Having been raised in "put it into them" missiology, it took a while for me fully to embrace the Quaker alternative. I had it figured out in theory, but I wasn't sure how it might work in practice. The turning point came when I tried to teach a dozen or so native Alaskans the "one right way" to lead a person to Christ. You see, I knew that way. I'd taught it for years to groups of volunteer children's workers all over America. It was something I had learned in Bible college and had regularly reinforced in ministry training with a worldwide missionary agency that specialized in winning children to Christ. When I was asked to teach an Alaska Bible Institute class on leading a person to Christ, I came with my tried-and-true notes and the full expectation that students would leave prepared to inject Christ into anyone they met. Boy, did I learn a lesson.

Every other time I'd taught the course, I'd begun with basic principles of evangelism as I understood them. Once they had those principles down, then the students would practice them on each other. *Dragnet's* Sgt. Friday would have loved me. I presented "just the facts." But this time was different. On a whim (an unQuakerly term for leading), I began by asking the students to share their stories of how they came to Christ. I assumed I'd hear tales of how someone presented the facts about Jesus to them, how they were offered an opportunity to decide for themselves, and how someone knelt with them in prayer. It wasn't that way with me, but I figured I'd done it wrong. I fully expected my students to get it right.

The first student to speak told of various encounters with God and God's people over the course of many years. Each encounter changed him a little and moved him farther along his spiritual path, but he couldn't point to one cataclysmic event that left him converted. Heads nodded in agreement. Then another student spoke, and she also pointed to numerous places where, looking back, she could see God's movement in her life. Again, no date of conversion to mark in their Bibles, just a solid faith that God was working in them and not yet finished.

Over and over these Bible Institute students told how they'd spent a lifetime coming closer to a God who'd been with them all along. Only two could relate traditional conversion experiences, and even they recognized it was a process begun before they were aware of their spiritual needs. Finally, I felt safe enough to share my story.

I was raised in a home and a church that placed a premium on instantaneous, miraculous conversion. The greater the life-change, the better. But I was a pretty good kid. I didn't do drugs. I didn't smoke or drink. I generally obeyed my parents. My mom had a little blue New Testament with a date written inside the front cover. It was the Rally Day at Grace Church when I was five and went forward in response to an evangelist. I have no recollection of the event.

I do remember the evening shortly before my twelfth birthday when I felt an overwhelming sense of "lostness" or "aloneness" as I ran outside to play with my friends. Instead of crossing the street to the stoop where the 93rd Street Gang was hanging out, I ran behind my house and crouched under the kitchen window where no one could see from inside or outside.

I prayed a real come-to-Jesus prayer and then felt good enough to join my friends. A few years later, I responded again to an invitation, this time to tell God I really meant business when it came to serving the Lord. A few years later I answered a call to water baptism, but that may have been to impress a girl at Bible college.

As I told my story, understanding heads among the Alaskan students nodded. They knew the feeling of multiple contact points with God along the spiritual journey. Even the two who could connect a date and time to their conversion recognized that God had always been working in them. So instead of teaching them a tried-and-true formula for making believers, we explored together how we can help people recognize the work of God in their lives and respond in joyful participation to whatever that work is. And that is the Quaker way of evangelism. It's not that we discount those glorious conversion experiences; it's just that we recognize them as one way among many that God connects with the people God created.

So what does a Friends pastor do when it comes to evangelism? Before I share some examples, let's look at my story from another perspective. What if you were a Quaker pastor who met me at some point along my journey? What would you have done? You might have celebrated, along with my mother, my excitement at hearing about Jesus and wanting to trust in him. You might have talked with me about why I wanted my relationship with God to be a private matter when I was a preteen. Or maybe you'd share your own story of a time when you felt lost or alone. Maybe you'd encourage me to find a place of service either in the church or in the community. You would meet me at exactly the place I was, identify with me there, help me to see God there, and celebrate the fact that God wasn't finished with either of us. You would, in the words of George Fox, "answer that of God" in me.

It's no wonder Fox prefaced his famous words with a reminder to "walk cheerfully." Who could not be cheerful when walking in a world where God appears all over the place? Where Martin Luther, in *A Mighty Fortress*, envisioned a devil-filled world threatening to undo us, the Friends pastor sees a world where God is constantly on the move, in the details and in the big picture, always finding ways to break in and surprise the expectant observer. It makes for a very cheerful outlook.

One evening I was home alone and noticed some Facebook postings commemorating the death of Christian singer-songwriter Rich Mullins, whom I'd met a few times over the years. I decided to watch a few YouTube videos of his performances. I was watching Rich sing *Sometimes by Step*, one of my favorites, when an instant message window opened on my computer. "Hi, Uncle Phil!" came the cheerful words of a young Egyptian friend, "How are you?"

I explained to my friend that I was both happy and sad at the moment. When she asked why, I told her I had been watching music videos by an old friend who had died some years ago. She asked if we could watch one together and opened a video sharing window. Together we watched the *Sometimes by Step* video. Mullins' lyrics washed over us:

> Oh God, You are my God, and I will ever
>   praise You
> I will seek You in the morning
> And I will learn to walk in Your ways

And step by step You'll lead me
And I will follow You all of my days[2]

When it was over, my friend, a devout Muslim, said, "Oh, Uncle Phil, that is what I believe." Over the years, my Egyptian friend and I have had some deep theological discussions where our differences come out clearly, and where we agree to disagree. But at that moment, that of God in each of us was calling out. We both heard it. And it was wonderful.

You never know at what place in their spiritual journey those you meet might be or where God might show up at any time. Sometimes even Quaker pastors are amazed.

I enjoy listening to what I call "melodic metal" music, although it has also been called "goth metal" and other names. I'll let music critics fight the semantic battles. I often participate in chatrooms with other, mostly younger, fans of various groups. It was in one such chatroom I met a young woman named Carol. She often wrote scathing criticisms of religion, Christianity in particular. She self-identified as a Satan worshiper. Nevertheless, we like some of the same bands, so we could be online friends.

One day, Carol wrote some very disturbing things about her life. Her mood, which was usually pretty dark—to match her black outfits—seemed to be veering toward a danger zone. I was concerned, and I sent her a private message with some words of encouragement. She immediately messaged me back. We began chatting, and she told me more about her religious views. At some point I mentioned how I believed she had some wonderful gifts and I could see her in ministry someday. She wrote back, "Really? My grandma says that too.

Do you really think it's true?" I assured her it was and suddenly our conversations became about God, not the glories of the devil or the evils of the church.

Sadly, I lost track of Carol over the years. I wouldn't be surprised to see her in a seminary class one day. Answering that of God in someone may mean listening past the spoken words and hearing what is in the heart. Friends pastors try to do that.

Because Friends believe God is always at work in people, even those whose faith—or lack thereof—is not described in the same terms as their own, the Quaker pastor may be more likely to engage in what academics call "interfaith dialog." I sometimes wonder about that term. I once spent a week at an interfaith conference surrounded by liberal Protestants listening to lectures mostly by other liberal Protestants, plus a Buddhist, a Jew, and a Sikh. Were it not for an afterhours ping-pong game with the Sikh, I'd have spent no time at all that week in real interfaith *dialog*, only interfaith monolog.

Friends are uniquely positioned for true dialog with persons of other faith traditions. We expect God to be in the conversation already. We know the presence of God is active within us, and we understand God to be actively present in the "other" as well. This doesn't mean we deny what we believe in deference to what others believe. I've found that interfaith relationships often grow stronger when each person feels free to express their beliefs and even defend them, knowing that the other person enjoys that same freedom of expression. Sometimes, maybe most of the time, both believers draw closer to God.

My travels in "answering that of God" have taken me to some wonderful places to meet some wonderful people. One time a Muslim gentleman from Turkey contacted the Quaker Information Network to learn more about Quakerism. He had studied Sufism and wanted to explore how the mystical side of Christianity, which he took to be Quakerism, compares. Since I had a trip to Turkey planned anyway, I added a visit to his home.

After a lovely dinner the first evening, as he showed me my guest room, my host said, "Tomorrow morning at nine o'clock we will have a Quaker meeting." And we did. We sat in silence, worshiping God, and then my friend spoke words from a vision he received. They were words of wisdom for both of us, and I believe they came from God.

I visited that man and his wife a year later. This time, after dinner and some television, my friend said, "Let's pray. Phil, would you lead us?" After some silence, I prayed the same kind of prayer I would pray among friends, or Friends, at home. I was talking to God in the only way I know with a rather decidedly Christian prayer. What a joy it was to hear my host respond, "Amen," when I was finished. When that man and I get together, God is there. I feel honored to be welcomed into his home, to be heard when I speak of my relationship with God, and to be in a position to listen to his experiences with God. We both grow in grace.

Answering that of God in others can bring a bit of heartbreak along with joy. When we speak of a relationship with God that is very important to us, we want to share it with those we care about. As Christians, we often consider only the giving part, not the receiving part. But answering "that of God" means receiving as well. And it may mean we will never share the exact same God experiences with other persons. That's not always easy to take or even easy to understand, and yet it follows a movement of the Spirit that goes beyond my religion or your religion.

My young Egyptian friend is, as I mentioned, a devout follower of Allah in the ways of Islam. Sometimes when we talk, I think I know what it is like to be on the receiving side of evangelism. I remember one particularly long conversation we had about God and Jesus and Muhammad and pigs. It was a conversation that focused more on our differences than on our manifestations of faith. At one point, my friend said, "Uncle Phil, you love God so much. Why are you not a Muslim?" It was a valid evangelistic question. I responded, "Because I found God through Jesus Christ, and I am happy to know God that way. You have found God through the teaching of the Prophet, and you are happy. I will not ask you to change, but I do not think I will ever change either." She was quiet for a few moments, and then she said, "Then I guess we will always disagree." I said, "I think so." She replied, "But you will always be my uncle." And I said, "Yes, I will always be your uncle."

When the Friends pastor is acting as an evangelist, she needs to be ready, as the Bible says, "to give an answer to everyone who asks you to give the reason for the hope that you have" (1 Peter 3:15 NIV). But she will be answering those in whom she believes God is already moving and drawing to Godself. It is a walk we take together with other people, not a set of principles we try to hammer into someone else's brain.

One of the tricky parts about the Quaker way of evangelism is when you walk cheerfully into an atheist. How does the Quaker pastor answer that of God in someone who denies the existence of such a Being? Just as I was about to record my words of wisdom on this subject, I realized I don't have any words of wisdom on this subject. I've never been an atheist. God has been a recognized part of my life since I first appeared in a church a week or two after I was born. Although I have occasional doubts, I couldn't even pass for an agnostic. But I do count agnostics and atheists among my dearest friends, and I do believe there is "that of God" in them, even if they don't. So I asked a few of these friends the following question:

> Unlike many Christians, who think God is something you need to inject into someone, Quakers believe there is "that of God in everyone." So, I often see what I would describe as God working in and through people who deny or question the existence of God. My question to you, an atheist [or agnostic], is, How do you react to my claiming to see God in you?

First of all, none of my friends were put off by my seeing God in them. They know I believe in God, and whether they consider such belief naïve, ill-informed, or superstitious, they recognize that it is genuine, and they respect that. One musician friend, an agnostic, introduced me to some folks in a pub as "the only Christian I know who thinks." So what does *he* think? Here's his reply: "'There are more things in heaven and earth than are dreamt of in my philosophy.' I'm a skeptical positivist, so I'm grateful. To you; not to a likely superstition."

I made this friend blush, he said, when I mentioned some particularly godly qualities I've observed in him. Is this "answering that of God"? Maybe not. It was a conversation begun solely for the purpose of writing this book. Still, I've spent hours in pubs with this friend, and with his friends and acquaintances. Over the years, conversations have turned from international politics to music to religion and, yes, to God. I can think of no time when God was not present for the discussion. I don't mind telling folks that, but I don't expect them all to agree.

What I do expect in conversation with persons who question or reject the existence of God is to be challenged to think. Maybe that's where God is when we talk with atheists and agnostics. Maybe the God who created our minds is fully present only when we are using them. This brings me to a conversation I had via Facebook chat with an atheist friend of mine, Marty. I asked my usual question (above), but he was not content to provide a simplistic answer. I will reproduce his response verbatim and then give my feelings and reply to him. He wrote,

> Hey Phil, I guess there are two answers to your question. The first easy one is simply I don't see God in me. But the other answer, which I guess would suit your inquiry better, is what is it specifically that you define [as] God? If you explain further about what is it that you see in people that you call it God, I might be able to give you a better answer. Right now off the cuff, if you define God as source of all goodness, I would say I consider it the in-built morality that for example makes me do good to others or help them, and do all the good things. It is totally unrelated to the binary oppositions in our culture such as God/Devil, Heaven/Hell, etc.

At the risk of revealing my philosophical shallowness, as well as my personal take on some historical Quaker beliefs, I will share my response:

> It is difficult to name a single god-like quality in any person. I could say I sense God in your honesty, your commitment to inquiry, and your love of knowledge, but that is simply naming qualities I admire. That's not really what I mean.

> At the moment, I am sitting at a table in a pub in Sidney, Nebraska, a place I've never been before. I am surrounded by strangers. I look at the man two tables over. He is gesturing with his finger like he is making a point to his friend. Even though I don't know him, and might not like him if I did, I believe there is a core in him that is divine. No, it's more than that. Maybe it is that I believe God is seated at that table, and at my table, and standing behind the bar. I guess I see the essence of human-ness is godness. Of course we have ways of obscuring it in ourselves and ignoring it in others.

> And I don't believe in the kind of binary opposites you mention. If there is a God, then that God has no equal opposite.

This prompted more discussion, first from Marty:

> Based on what you have said, I guess we both agree on certain things, and the only difference is that we have different names for them. I personally believe that every word has a weight,

in other words there are several implications/
associations with words that are not possible
to be overlooked. Then again morality and
human-ness have less association in my
opinion, and this makes them better terms.
For instance you don't need to believe in God
to be a good person; however, a belief/disbelief
in God makes it possible for people to brand
each other. This branding/categorizing can lead
to various results. In the previous centuries it
could be used by corrupt leaders to encourage
the believers to kill the non-believers, and in our
day and age, despite various religiously induced
terrorist attacks, has been toned down and
become milder. However, it exists. However,
when I say human goodness, or humanness, it
would be much harder to make a case for killing
others according to this term. I don't know
whether I am beating around the bush or not,
but let me know if this is what you wanted to
discuss originally.

And then from me:

I'm going to give my perspective which is both
theist and Christian, although I suspect some of
my fellow Christians would not agree.

While I believe God and God's creation are not
one and the same, I do think they are irrevocably
connected, that "image of God" thing in the
Hebrew scriptures. But, contrary to those who
see humankind as totally depraved, I think our
essential humanness is what is most closely

related to God. When I preached through the New Testament Gospel of Mark a few years ago, I realized why Jesus referred to himself as "Son of Man" and not Son of God. He represented all that was best in humans, and that also got him labeled "Son of God."

So, maybe Quakers see a person's essential humanness first, and that makes them recognize God in people. Again, people—all of us—often mask that divine essence with self- and species-destructive thoughts and behavior.

Let me reiterate here that I am not trying to play the philosopher. You and I probably disagree on many points of theology, and we may agree on many more. I share these stories as an example of what "answering that of God" looks like in real life with real people who do not subscribe to the same belief system we do. Marty is not going to convert me to atheism. I likely will not convert him to Christianity, although one time he did say to me, "One of these days you might get me to become a Quaker." However, there is something wholesome, invigorating, and life-affirming when we view a conversation with the "other" as an opportunity for mutual growth—yes, even spiritual growth—when that of God in me answers that of God in someone else.

So what is the Quaker pastor's role in all this? First, I believe we need to set an example for our meetings. We need to walk that cheerful path to the best of our Spirit-inspired ability. And we should, with Quakerly humility, share our stories with our meetings.

Second, we Friends pastors should encourage our meetings to expect godly encounters in our daily lives.

One way to do that is to celebrate those encounters when we hear about them from our congregants. Give your meeting members the opportunity to tell their stories in meeting. Maybe take a few moments each week for an "answering that of God" testimony time. We won't have those encounters if we don't look for them; and we won't look for them if we aren't reminded that they are waiting for us.

Last we, and our meetings, need to remember that for some people the next step on their spiritual journey may be with us. Friends too often are timid about sharing the good news they have found in their relationship with God. Engaging in dialog with others is fun and enlightening, but sometimes our faith story is the gospel someone else is waiting for. Answering that of God in others means bearing witness to that of God in us. Tactfully, of course. Without coercion, of course. But if we are to give full respect to the people we meet, and that of God in them, then we must give an honest account of that of God in us as well.

Sometimes, of course, answering that of God in those outside the church is easier than seeing that of God in some religious folk. One place where the challenge is greatest is within the confines of the church boardroom. Yet for the Friends pastor, if we cannot see God at work among our closest spiritual neighbors, how can we truly answer that of God in the "other?"

# ▪ 6 ▪

## Are We There Yet?
## The Friends Pastor and Church Administration

Remember those long—interminably long—rides when you were a kid? The ride to Grandma's house for Christmas gift giving. The ride to the beach for a weekend of sun and water fun. The vacation trip to Florida, California, or Tennessee. What question was foremost in your mind and often on your lips? *Are we there yet?* As a parent and grandparent I've heard the words "are we there yet" more times than I can remember.

Some years ago, I heard those words "are we there yet" in an entirely different context, and it changed my way of thinking about making important decisions. You might say it "convinced" me of the Quaker way of doing business. Oddly enough, it was not at a Quaker meeting, and the one whose leadership brought about my convincement was not part of the Society of Friends.

In the early 1990s, I was part of a team, comprised of Brethren, Mennonites, Friends, and others, that developed the *Jubilee: God's Good News* curriculum for children. Rosella Wiens Regier, a Mennonite educator, chaired the group.

Bringing together seven denominations, even those linked in the historic peace church traditions, was bound to elicit some disagreement regarding how to design a Christian education curriculum. It was up to Rosella to see that every person's voice was heard, every group's theological nuances were respected, and above all, that the curriculum would help guide children in exploring the Bible in a way that was meaningful to them.

I remember one of the first meetings. There were about fifteen of us sitting around a square of tables. We had reached a critical point in that stage of our work. There were voices expressing certain ideas while other voices rejected or modified those ideas.

Rosella stood at the front of the room with a blue marker in her hand. Behind her was a large erasable marker board. She listened to the discussion taking place around the tables. Every so often she would stop the conversation, write on the board and say, "Is this what we mean?" There would be some agreement along with a few people saying, "No," or, "Well, not exactly." Then we'd talk some more, fine tuning Rosella's interpretation of what the group was thinking.

After a while, Rosella would rewrite, tweak, or amend what was on the board. Once again, she'd ask, "Is this what we mean?" Again the group would respond, usually with more agreement but maybe a few "not exactlys." We'd resume our conversation, but with an even sharper focus, and Rosella would listen and then write what she was hearing into the words on the board. "Are we there yet?" she'd ask. Yes, we were closer, but not quite.

Finally, after a few more minutes of discussion and maybe one or two more "are we there yets," the smiles would appear. We were there. Rosella had accurately discerned and articulated what the group of educators around the tables was saying. The words on the board became part of the foundation for the new curriculum. And we were ready to move on to the next stage of development.

Although I'd been a Friends pastor and Christian educator for six years, it wasn't until I attended those curriculum development meetings that I began to understand what clerking (like chairing, but in Quakerese and with a more spiritual bent) a meeting was all about. When it comes to what is traditionally known as church administration and the Friends pastor's relationship to it, I believe we need to begin with the meeting for business and the role of the clerk. After that, we can see where pastors fit in.

Meeting for worship for the purpose of business is at the core of Quaker church administration because it stems directly from Friends theology, particularly the fundamental belief that the living Christ is present in the meeting and that all persons at that meeting are equals. When I questioned Friends pastors about Quaker business, one Evangelical Friends Church pastor described it like this:

> Quaker polity, properly applied, is unlike the administration of any other denomination. Truly following the Spirit by the consensus of the congregation requires unity of patience, unity of understanding, total openness to the Spirit and to one another, and many other gifts. The Quaker pastor must balance directive ministry that comes from the leading of the Spirit with the ministry of every believer (also of the Holy Spirit). The Friends pastor may feel limited by the process of consensus but at the same time must realize the potential of the ministry of the entire congregation.

The word "consensus" leads one to think of absolute unanimity in decision making, which doesn't quite describe the process by which Friends decide their business. Michael Birkel gives a more succinct description of Quaker business process in his chapter on "Leadings and Discernment" in *The Oxford Handbook of Quaker Studies*. He begins by saying,

> When Friends gather in what they call Meeting for Business to consider and decide about practical matters, they practice corporate discernment. In Meeting for Worship Friends have historically experienced a powerful sense of unity; likewise when they gather to attend to business, they aspire to unity. Majority rule therefore does not suffice, so they do not vote in Meetings for Business. Instead, they wait for "the sense of the meeting"; a decision in which all present can come to unity.[1]

The unity Birkel mentions is not necessarily unanimity, and somewhere in the process someone present at the meeting must discern the point when the sense of the meeting is achieved. That someone is the clerk. Whether they are the clerk or chairperson of a sub-committee or the clerk of a monthly, quarterly, or yearly meeting, it is the clerk who leads the meeting. Pastors in most Friends meetings do play a part, which I will discuss later in this chapter, but they are not the primary authority in the meeting.

Actually, the clerk isn't the authority either, at least not in the "boss" manner of thinking. The clerk may work with others to set a meeting's agenda, but her or his job is to discern God's leading for the entire group.

An important part of this process is making sure every voice is heard that wants to be heard. In this way, within those voices, the clerk hopes to hear God speak, which brings us back to that centuries-old idea of "that of God" in everyone.

Quaker pastors work in a setting where our voice is but one through whom God may speak. We, like every member of the meeting, seek to be in close enough communion with God that God's voice is clearly discerned. Sometimes, however, we can be surprised when God seems to be telling people something we think might be a little crazy.

In 2014, I had the privilege of teaching at the Cuban Quaker Institute of Peace in Gibara, Cuba. In one of the classes we were talking about the ways Friends listen to the Spirit's leading in matters of church business. A student, Sofia, recounted a story of a time when the Spirit led in a way that caused her—the pastor— to wonder if this listening for God's voice thing really made sense. It illustrates how discerning God's voice is a community process for Friends and not simply a "well, I heard God tell me..." thing.

Sofia related that a recent hurricane had destroyed the roof of one of the members of her Friends meeting. The woman had no place to live or store her few household items safely. During meeting for worship, Sofia brought the matter up for discussion. She felt the meeting should do something to help Sara as soon as possible. According to Sofia,

> We began to think about the different options, and one of them was to use funds from the treasury of the monthly meeting. I resisted this option, thinking that it was unwise, too fast,

and that it would bring difficulties because it would take the funds from the other scheduled activities.[2]

The meeting for worship continued as an impromptu meeting for business as Friends in attendance voiced their leadings on the matter. Sofia tried to think of ways to stop what she perceived to be an illogical idea. She told the people they were too busy and too poor to begin such a building project. Friends replied that they had enough money in their bank account and that there was a large segment of time each week when all the members of the meeting were available: Sunday mornings.

The meeting continued with times of silent waiting and periods of vocal ministry. Logic, at least in human terms, dictated prudence and fiscal responsibility—and that voice was heard. But other voices were heard as well, and among them was God's. After much waiting and much discussion, the clerk knew what the right decision was. The meeting would gather up *all* of its meager finances and invite all of its members to a series of Sunday morning meetings for construction. They even hung a sign on the door of the meetinghouse. It said, simply, "Worship is being held in rebuilding Sara's house."

What happened in that Cuban town is the essence of Quaker church administration. There was leadership in the form of the meeting clerk and the pastor, but neither one asserted their authority out of place. The pastor played no "I'm your spiritual leader" card. The clerk didn't force his agenda on the meeting. Everyone was willing to listen for the Spirit's leading in this very difficult decision. Timing seemed crucial. After all, a woman's health and safety were at stake. But the meeting took the time it needed to listen. Money mattered. There is never enough to go around in Cuba. But the meeting was willing to entertain the outrageous idea of using their savings to renovate someone else's building.

I appreciate Sofia's part in the story. She began as an opponent of the original idea of using meeting funds to help one person. Pastors have every right to oppose or support ideas brought forth in business meetings. They are part of the meeting, too. But Sofia did not use her pastoral position to force the meeting's decision. No matter how crazy the idea seemed to her, she was willing to listen, along with the other meeting members, for the voice of God.

So what *is* the role of the Friends pastor in church administration?

First, we are part of the meeting. We can have our say in meetings where we sit as members, whether ex officio or by appointment or nomination. We speak and listen as equals with every other member of that meeting or committee.

This isn't always easy to do. Many Friends pastors come from faith traditions where pastors have a higher degree of positional authority. Some congregations have many members who come from a hierarchical form of governance. Where that is the case, the idea of listening for the voice of someone who doesn't even appear to be present at the meeting seems daunting, if not ludicrous. But the old *Presence in the Midst* painting is there to remind us that Christ *is* present. We pastors can do a great service for our congregations if we set the example of waiting and listening for, as well as preaching about, the active presence of the Christ in our meetings.

Second, we are given a certain amount of authority by the meeting, and that is in the area of spiritual guidance. Pastors are expected to be leaders when it comes to assisting the spiritual formation of local Friends. We exercise this leadership when we preach and teach. We exercise this leadership when we give spiritual direction to individuals and groups. We can exercise this leadership in areas of business as well.

I used to feel out of place as an ex officio member of the Ministry and Oversight Committee in meetings I pastored. What was my function? I wasn't there for financial direction or business wisdom. My ideas about the annual pig roast or the theme of our Heritage Days float were no better or more important than anyone else's. Mine was just another voice, and not the most learned one, in most church business.

Then one day I asked myself what exactly *was* my place in these meetings. The answer hit me with the hammer blow of obviousness: *I was the pastor.* I was the pastor not only in the pulpit or in my office or in the hospital. I was the pastor in the business meeting. From then on, I decided to act like it.

Before the next Ministry and Oversight meeting at the church I was pastoring at that time, I spoke with the clerk about how I wanted to be present at the next committee meeting. I said I wanted not just to give the opening and closing prayers but to start with a time of reflection on how we, as individuals on a committee, had been seeing God at work in our meeting or in our lives. I hoped to use my pastoral authority to assist the committee in recognizing the presence of God in everything we do. I thought if we could do that, then listening for God when it came time to make decisions would be more natural.

It worked! As I found my place in the meeting, all the other members began to see their places as well and to understand that theirs was not just a name on a list, but that they were functioning channels of the Spirit. From then on, the clerk would begin the meeting and then turn it over to me for some, shall we say, group spiritual direction before we attended to business decisions.

Third, because we are among equals, our ideas have equal validity with others in the meeting or committee. This is not always easy to carry out in practice. Many of us "Friendly" pastors bend toward passivity. We hesitate to put forth our own ideas, deferring to the lay ministers most of the time. While this may seem like a way to encourage the ministry of all believers, it may deprive an important decision of key information only the pastor can provide. Of course, even when we are so bold as to inject our ideas, there is no guarantee we'll be heard.

Prior to seminary and before I took to the pulpit, my background was in Christian education. I had directed day camps, trained Sunday school teachers, served as a local director of an international children's mission organization, and was a children's pastor in a medium-large congregation. I'm not even counting the decades spent teaching Sunday school and children's church or serving on Christian education committees. By the time I became a preaching minister, I had a pretty good knowledge of things related to church education.

Was I ever excited when the church I was pastoring decided it was time to replace the room dividers in the basement education room. You know those rooms: big multi-purpose creatures that can be turned from a fellowship hall to classrooms by sliding a few accordion-style doors. Well, I knew those doors. I'd helped a church shop for them before. I'd served in churches with various kinds of folding doors. I knew doors, (expletive)!

During a Ministry and Oversight meeting, I ventured beyond my role as spiritual guide and offered a comment about the doors under consideration. I spoke with the confidence of years of experience, knowing that my suggestion could save the meeting a lot of future frustration if they chose the wrong doors. I had barely finished presenting my ideas when the clerk of the committee reminded me in no uncertain terms that I was the pastor and had nothing to say when it came to big-ticket purchases of church furnishings.

I took my censure quietly, hoping the meeting would make the best decision even without my input. And when I teach the Church Administration class at Earlham School of Religion, I remind students that as pastors they are not likely to be appreciated for any expertise beyond theology. Still, I question my silence at that meeting after offering my suggestion. Was I wrong to assert my authority, not as pastor but as an experienced folding-door-shopper and user? I don't think so. Sometimes we pastors just know stuff, and like any other church member or board member we have the right, even the responsibility, to share what we know if it will help the church. How we share it, whether with humility or arrogance, that's up to us. How it is received, well, sometimes that is out of our hands.

Last, there are times, often at denominational or ecumenical meetings, when we are called on to clerk or preside over a meeting. That's when our knowledge of Quaker practice and our recollection of times we saw it done right comes in handy.

During my years as Christian Education Consultant for Evangelical Friends International-North American Region, I spent a lot of time in meetings with representatives of the denominations with whom Friends worked on curriculum development. While most of the meetings were chaired by members of the lead publishing denomination, subcommittee meetings could be led by folks from any of the partnership members.

One year, I was asked to chair a sub-committee developing a new preschool curriculum. We hit what seemed to be an impenetrable wall when we tried to decide how or whether to teach Jesus' miracle stories to four- and five-year-olds. Hours of debate had brought us no nearer to a resolution and the afternoon was drawing to a close. I remember wondering how we could ever move from such a heated discussion to a cordial and fun time of fellowship at dinner. So I played my Quaker card.

You might remember, there's really no such thing as a Quaker card. We can't simply inject some Quakerly tidbit into a conversation or meeting and expect everyone to stop, listen, and humbly obey. However, in those times when we Quaker pastors have leadership roles in non-Quaker settings, suggesting a Friendly way of doing business can lead to a refreshing new way of reaching a goal.

What I did in my role as sub-committee chair was to end the discussion at that point, about forty-five minutes before we were to go out for dinner. Admitting we were not close to reaching an acceptable decision, I asked the group to go back to their rooms and spend half an hour in prayer about the key questions with which we'd been dealing. Then, I told them, lay it all aside and get ready for dinner. Let's have some fun tonight. I added that after dinner they should spend some more time in prayer before going to bed. Then, I said, let's see where we are in the morning.

Apparently, the committee took what I said to heart. We had a wonderfully relaxed dinner at a fine restaurant and plenty of good, non-work-related conversation over coffee. I returned to our meeting room well in advance of our morning meeting. I wanted some quiet time of my own. At 9:00 a.m. the group reconvened.

I won't reveal how we resolved the issue, a) because it is a discussion more suited to a religious education class or a theology pub, and b) because I don't remember. What I do remember is convening the meeting with a period of silent worship. Then I asked each person in the group, in turn, counter-clockwise around the tables, to share their thoughts on our subject.

As we listened to each other's ideas, we all started sensing something was happening. There wasn't total unanimity, but there was harmony in our positions. I sensed we had reached a point of resolution. Everyone else sensed it, too. You could tell by the smiles that started appearing.

After everyone had spoken, I said, "I think we have our position on Jesus' miracles for this curriculum." I stated it, and everyone agreed. Instead of spending the morning in heated debate, we stood for a circle of praise and worship, and then we knocked off for an hour while the other committees sorted through their issues.

I'm not saying that Friends have the only right way of doing church business. And I've seen Quaker process abused by lovers of power and by passive aggressiveness. But when it is used to really listen for the voice of that ever-present Christ and to respond to *His* leadership, not the pastor's or the clerk's, then amazing things can happen. And we Friends pastors are part of that process. This kind of listening does not come naturally, at least for most of us, which is why we need to teach it in our churches. In more than one way, the sense of church being a place where God is actively present forms the basis of another aspect of pastoral ministry: religious education.

# ▪ 7 ▪

## Making Room for the Teacher:
## The Friends Pastor and Religious Education

**M**aggie had prepared a wonderful lesson for her combined first- through fourth-grade Sunday school class. She always did. She was very organized in her preparation and very creative in her lesson design. Her dozens of years of experience with children had taught her most of what she needed to know about learning and classroom management. However, this particular Sunday morning, nothing was working. She just couldn't seem to get through to them the wonderful truths of the Bible.

On this day, Maggie had to draw on a resource they don't keep in church supply closets. She tried something so audacious that it stunned her students and teaching partner alike. She invited the students to sit on the floor with her, if they weren't sitting there already, and she apologized for losing control of the classroom. Then she asked the students to pray with her that the Spirit would gather the class so that learning and fun could happen.

Maggie and the kids stayed there, sitting on the floor, praying silently, until a spirit of calm prevailed. At a time when I'm sure many teachers would have exerted control by tightening the reins, Maggie gave up control, not to disruptive students, but to a peacemaking spirit. She did what Friends do. She made room for the Teacher.

"The Lord Christ Jesus was come to teach his people himself," so George Fox told a group of church folk at Sedbergh, England, in 1652.[1] More than 350 years later, this simple saying has become the foundation of Quaker religious education. However, it raises a serious question. Who needs classrooms, curricula, and teachers when all you have to do is wait for the heavenly Teacher to show up? Then again, isn't that what Friends do in worship? Is the Friendly view of education an act of worship or learning or both? And what are the roles of the pastor and the teacher in all this?

Here again we find the *Presence in the Midst* that is so much a part of who Friends are. The Quaker pastor doesn't teach the things she or he has studied, although study should never be neglected; the Quaker pastor teaches people to listen for the voice of the One who teaches them from within. A yearly meeting superintendent expressed it like this, "George Fox observed that his role as a minister was to bring people to the feet of Christ, our teacher."

Regarding the ministry of teaching, a Friends pastor I surveyed said,

> For Friends, learning is a community process. Teaching is a cooperative undertaking to assist people in learning that can take many forms. As I understand Friends, learning is seen as a discovery process that grows out of interactions with the Spirit, the Bible, and community. This sets us apart from those that focus on learning as transmitting truth. We have truth, but it is discovered, not transmitted.

On the surface, the above paragraph sounds like little more than someone equating sound educational theory with Quaker process. However, I think there is more to it. Friends are most Friendly when in community. We speak of the "gathered meeting" where Christ is present. We do business according to the sense of the meeting, which is ascertained when all voices are heard and the clerk seeks to know God's will for the community. The Quaker teacher recognizes that his or her words are only part of the learning process. The Spirit within the hearts of the learners and the teacher will guide Friends "into all truth," as Jesus promised (John 16:13). Just as Friends discern God's will in community, so they discern truth in community.

Parker Palmer, a Quaker educator who is highly regarded far beyond the Society of Friends for recognizing teaching as a spiritual experience, elaborates on his educational philosophy in *To Know as We Are Known*. In it he creates and dissects a simple definition: to teach is to create a space in which obedience to truth is practiced.[2] This, I believe, is where the work of the Friends pastor comes in. If we truly believe in the presence of the Teacher in our churches and meetings, then it becomes our job to create a welcome for Him. Fortunately, Friend Palmer gives us some guidance for this process. He mentions three criteria: openness, boundaries, and hospitality. Openness creates a safe space for people to leave their comfort zone; boundaries keep them focused while still allowing the Teacher to move among them; and hospitality welcomes the voice of the stranger, through whom the Teacher may speak to us.

Openness is a commodity too often lacking in churches. We enjoy hiding our real selves behind walls of niceness, smiles, and pleasantries. The irony is that, for most of us, spiritual growth seems to come only after periods of crisis. Consider when you began your faith journey. If your religious background is anything like mine, you came to a point in your life where you realized you could not save yourself. Something inside was hindering your relationship with God. Call it sin, call it self, call it anything you want: it was eating at you and you could not move forward spiritually until you recognized it was there and turned to God for healing, for relief, for salvation. The crisis moved you forward in your spiritual development. From there you rested and then renewed your journey, slowly, until another crisis of faith entered your life. Once again you turned to God and in the midst of the struggle found something that brought you to a deeper level of faith. That's generally the way faith develops. We grow, we face a crisis, we admit that we cannot master the situation on our own, we turn to God, and we grow some more. Right in the middle of all that is vulnerability. And we can't move forward without it.

Openness is the first part of creating a welcome for the Teacher. Openness happens when, in communion with other people, we admit to the struggles that have formed our spiritual growth. Then, together with others who are on the same journey, we "grow in grace" (2 Peter 3:18).

The problem is most churches are more closed than open. We dare not reveal any weaknesses to those around us. Why are we so closed to one another? I think  it has to do with safety. We just don't feel safe enough to reveal our deepest needs in church. By shutting ourselves off this way, we remain in a constant state of inertia: no forward movement, no growth, no spiritual development.

Not only does closing ourselves off stifle our own spiritual development, it takes away opportunities for other members of the community to grow. Ultimately, it shuts out the One who is our source of spiritual life, the Teacher.

So what can a Friends pastor do to encourage openness in the educational ministries of their meeting? The quick answer is to create an atmosphere of safety, but that is not so easy. At least it wasn't for me. I have never been a "touchy-feely" person. People say I used to visibly cringe when people hugged me. Then I was asked to teach a course called Christian Discipleship at George Fox University in Oregon. I followed the syllabus of Dr. Gary Fawver, who taught the other section of the popular course.

One of the most important parts of the course was the formation of discipling groups. These consisted of four or five students who would meet together for at least one hour weekly, on their own time, during the semester. They would set their own meeting time, location, and agenda. Only once during the semester would the professor attend. The goal of the groups was that at the end of the semester every class member would be able to say honestly, "I am a stronger Christian now than I was three months ago because of this group of people."

The question for Gary and me always was, how do you put these groups together? Do you let them pick their friends? No! I remember what it was like to be chosen last for schoolyard basketball games. Do you assign them to groups hoping it'll work out? No, because if they don't, all the blame falls on you. We chose Spirit-directed randomness as our method. We wanted to create a setting so safe for our students that it wouldn't matter with whom anyone was linked, even when dealing with issues that pushed them beyond their comfort zones.

So during the first three weeks of the course, class time was devoted almost exclusively to community-building activities. We played goofy games; we did a lot of discussion of personal issues in pairs and groups of three or four. We worked on building trust. Students never knew from one class to the next with whom they might be partnered for a game, a discussion, or a scavenger hunt. I think the enrollment was always so high because everyone who took it talked about how much fun we had during those weeks.

I remember the first semester I taught the class. At the end of the third week, I brought in a cooler of punch and a couple of trays of cupcakes with birthday candles on them. At the end of our class session, we lit the candles, and everyone picked a cupcake. One student asked, "Whose birthday are we celebrating?" I answered, "We're celebrating the birthday of our discipling groups. The color of your candle indicates what group you're in." No one was disappointed with their group. Everyone grew spiritually in that semester's class and in subsequent classes.

What was the secret to that class? Why were students so able to grow spiritually in their randomly selected groups? The answer is that the sense of safety developed in the classroom enabled the discipling groups to be open to themselves and to the Teacher no matter who was matched with whom.

I've continued to try making an open, safe community part of my educational practice, especially in courses like Introduction to Preaching, which can be very stressful for seminarians. During the years I team-taught the class with Dr. Dawn Ottoni-Wilhelm from Bethany Theological Seminary, we made sure the first few class sessions included plenty of opportunities for building community. We wanted the students to feel safe critiquing and being critiqued by their peers—in love. It worked beautifully. One year, however, due to the size of the class, we skipped the community building activities. During the semester, something felt wrong, smothered. At the end of the course, on the evaluations from the students, many commented that they didn't feel they could be honest in their critiques of each other's sermons because they didn't know each other well enough. The openness wasn't there. Guess what? Community building was back in the syllabus the next year, and the classes have been better for it. Openness creates space for the Teacher, and real learning happens.

I love the Sunday school class at Williamsburg Friends, where I pastored for seventeen years. Anita, the teacher, was always willing to question things. (She did the same as a public-school music and drama teacher for many years.) She'd ask for the "whys" of a scripture text. She never settled for face value. And she encouraged her students to do the same. She could do that because she was open with her students about her own questions and doubts. In doing so, she created a space where students could be honest about their spiritual lives. When that happens, and I know this from experience as Anita's student, the Teacher takes over.

Boundaries form the second part of a learning space that welcomes the Teacher. As open as we want our meetings and classrooms to be, there is always that possibility that openness will be an end in itself and not a part of the learning process. How many Sunday school classes have evolved into fellowship groups where learning has been sacrificed to good-to-be-here feelings? Palmer writes,

> The openness of a space is created by the firmness of its *boundaries*. A learning space cannot go on forever; if it did, it would not be a structure for learning but an invitation to confusion and chaos.[3]

For Friends who want to welcome the Teacher, the space must be open, but it must be within a sense of boundary. Religious education is not a free-for-all. It's hard to hear the Teacher when our minds, and sometimes our bodies, are running all over the place. The Quaker leader, be they classroom teacher or pastor in their preacher role, will learn to create boundaries wherein openness can be practiced and the Teacher can move among the students. The story I related about Maggie and her unruly class reminds me that boundaries are as important as openness in a Spirit-welcoming classroom.

Personally, I tend toward the openness part of the learning process. I want to leave lots of space for the Spirit to do the teaching. At the same time, I know that graduate students, especially Quaker graduate students, love to follow deer trails, chase rabbits, and generally wander while they remind us that "all who wander are not lost." Knowing, or at least strongly suspecting, that not all wandering equals listening to the Spirit, I try to make sure there are boundaries in place in my classrooms, be they real or virtual.

I like to create space for stimulating discussions in my classes. I assign reading material that—I hope—

stretches my students' perceptions about themselves, God, and theology. When we talk about it in class, I expect lively dialog as students talk about where they've been stretched and how they pushed back or welcomed new ideas. At the same time, somewhere out there, circling the classroom or online forum, is a fence, a boundary. You might not see it until you get really close, but it's there.

Some fences are like that. I remember when invisible fences were all the rage in suburban neighborhoods where people wanted to give the appearance of animals roaming free while insuring that their dogs didn't dig up someone's flower bed. These days, when I drive by our pasture at night, I can see the horses, but I don't always see the five strands of electric fence that keep them from wandering off. If, however, a passerby stopped to get a closer look, they'd see the fence before they felt it. Still, when a fence is further out and not close at hand, it may be difficult to see. One week, an online class discussion was ranging particularly far afield. One of the students remarked that it seemed we'd drifted too far away from the subject for that unit of instruction. I didn't have to write a response. Another student quickly replied, "Oh no! It may feel like we're completely lost, but Phil knows exactly where we're going to end up." I did have an idea of where I wanted the class to end up and would respond to their comments in such a way that it would gently lead them all toward the goal. The student who responded had sensed the unseen boundary, which gave the whole class the freedom to learn in their own way and from their own perspective, without having to worry whether their ideas were straying too far.

One might rightly ask, how does a teacher create such boundaries? How can students trust that their teacher has their best interests at heart by setting boundaries? These questions speak to curriculum, the plan by which we organize education. As a former religious education curriculum editor and writer, and as one who deals with syllabi, learning objectives, and lesson plans on a daily basis, I see curricula as a primary locus for creating healthy and helpful boundaries.

A few years ago, Earlham School of Religion (ESR) asked its faculty to create master syllabi for all their classes. A master syllabus is both specific and vague. It specifically states the desired objectives of the course as articulated by the primary instructor and approved by the faculty. However, master syllabi are designed to be used not just by full-time professors. The syllabus can be given to an adjunct who will design their own course, when called upon, using the same objective but making their own best choices for texts and methodology, resulting in freedom within established boundaries.

Moving from a macro level to the micro, each class session I teach is a boundary within a boundary. I write lesson plans in hopes of achieving a particular result. I write those plans based on course objectives approved in community—the seminary faculty—who rigorously, in the hope they are being guided by the Teacher, co-discern what the class should be like. Here again Friends return to their core beliefs: the present Teacher and the omnipresence of that Teacher in the world. Recognizing the immediate presence of the Teacher begins as we develop our curriculum and continues when we work through that plan in the classroom.

I bring the plan—the boundary—to class with two thoughts in mind: one, that the lesson plan contains a good idea of what might happen; and two, that the Teacher will take that lesson plan, use it, revise it, or subvert it, so that real spiritual development can take place.

With this second point in mind, I am constantly on the lookout for that overworked, yet supremely valued phrase all educators dream of: the teachable moment. Maggie saw one and grabbed it. Although most educators look for these, and one need not be Quaker or Christian or even theist to find them, I believe the Quaker educator, or the Friends pastor in their educator role, has a kind of home field advantage because they view the world as a community in which God's presence is constantly active. We plan in communion with the meeting, via religious education committees, teacher support groups, teaching team conversations over coffee; and then we carry out our plans (boundaries) in an atmosphere permeated by the Spirit, who is in every student and in their teachers.

Openness and boundaries reflect a Friendly way of education. To those, Palmer adds his third criterion for the learning process: hospitality. At first glance, it would seem hospitality is a lot like openness. Not quite, according to Palmer. The open classroom makes space for learning, but hospitality invites strangers into that space. Parker writes, "So the classroom where truth is central will be a place where every stranger and every strange utterance is met with welcome."[4] This returns to one of the essential practices of Friends, "answering that of God in everyone."

As a trained educator, this has been a difficult concept for me to incorporate into my lesson plans and practice. I learned in college the basic rules for curriculum design. I had years of practice designing "learning outcomes" and "evidences of learning." And as much as I like to talk about being student-focused, the center of the classroom is usually me. But in all my years of teaching, it is not the well-planned lessons that I remember, it is the times when some action or word burst into the class from someone other than me and acted as a catalyst for the learning I had hoped would take place. This is where hospitality comes in. Am I as a pastor/teacher willing to welcome that catalyst into my carefully crafted plan? Is my learning space hospitable to the voice of the stranger?

Palmer's concept of hospitality calls to mind the safety I mentioned earlier. People like to feel safe. Hospitality makes people feel safe. Were you to invite me into your home, you would make sure my needs are taken care of and that I feel comfortable and secure in your home and within your hospitality. Educational spaces need to be like that, but they also need to be more. If we are going to learn, to develop spiritually and mentally, we need to move beyond comfort.

Palmer reminds us that hospitality does not engender simply a feel-good educational venue; rather, it opens us up to pain. He writes,

> Hospitality is not an end in itself. It is offered for the sake of what it can allow, permit, encourage, and yield. A learning space needs to be hospitable not to make learning painless but to make the painful things possible, things like exposing ignorance, testing negative hypotheses, challenging false or partial information, and mutual criticism of thought.[5]

And it is in and through this pain that real transformative learning takes place. A painful period in American history may help us understand how this works: I grew up in an era where gas stations still had two sets of restrooms, and the ones labeled "whites only" were infinitely more pleasant than the others. My generation, me included, had to learn how wrong this was. Our development was stifled until we stretched ourselves to the point where *all* restrooms were clean and the segregationist labels came off the doors. That wasn't easy for us. Learning is hard. Sometimes it took people who weren't just like us—people willing to come into our lives through protest and challenge, whether in person or in the news—to make sure we learned.

I teach at a Quaker seminary that is partnered with a Church of the Brethren seminary next door. Brethren and Friends are among those who are known as historic peace churches. (Mennonites complete this trilogy.) Generally, Friends and Brethren are passive in their decision making, preferring to ruminate on an idea and draw everyone into the process before a decision is complete. We think that is a pretty good way of doing church business, as you might have surmised from a previous chapter in this book. Most of my students follow this laid back—wait-for-everyone-to-get-on-board—pattern of leading. It took a stranger to teach us that our way isn't the only way—maybe not even the only *right way*—of doing business.

One evening, my Church Administration class had a visitor. David was a leader in a local African American congregation, and he was considering seminary. Part of his tour of Earlham School of Religion included my class. That night we were talking about how, when initiating change in a congregation, it is good for leaders to work their vision through a congregation much the way a baker works yeast into dough. I lectured, with the total agreement of all my regular students, about how we spend time with different circles of influence relating our vision for the church and discerning together the will of God. Once all levels of leadership are convinced, we can make a decision.

David, our visitor, sat quietly through the lecture, his head occasionally turning side to side, but slowly, not wanting to upset the group. Finally, he could stand it no more. He raised his hand and after I acknowledged him, said, "Well, that's not how it is in my church! In my church, if the pastor has a vision from God, he just steps into the pulpit, tells us what the vision is, and we say 'Amen,' and we do it."

The class was shocked at first, and then the change took place. We began to realize that some Christians conduct church business in ways that are not the same as our dearly held beliefs, and that may not be wrong. David's church culture ceded more authority to the pastor, expecting the pastor to be led by God, which is somewhat similar to the way Friends and Brethren expect the presiding clerk and the congregation to be led by God. David's remark may have been a jolt to our system, but we left class that day a little more open to God. (By way of post script, David changed a bit too. He did attend and eventually graduate from ESR, and for a while he held a position at Earlham College, where he practiced a more Quaker style of decision making.)

In our religious education classrooms, we teach some difficult things to our students. We encourage them to experiment. We recognize that doubts may occur. To encourage this difficult learning, we need to become hospitable to different or difficult ideas and people. We need to consciously open our space with welcome for the stranger. We make it safe, but not so safe that stagnation sets in. Rather, we make it safe enough for us to leave our comfort zone. The visitor to our classroom, or the kid from whom you'd never expect a positive word, is welcomed in such a place. And we know that God is in them, so anything is possible.

My experiences have taught me that Parker Palmer captured essential aspects of the spiritually-grounded and -oriented learning environment: there must be openness, which creates a safe space for learning to take place; boundaries that help keep learners and teachers focused on the truth; and hospitality that welcomes the voice of the stranger through whom truth might come into the community and whose disruption of equilibrium could create the pain that pushes us toward transformation.

What then is the Friends pastor's role in such a distinctly, though not exclusively, Quaker educational process? I believe we are the doorkeepers. We are the ones who create the open space. Oh, we don't do it alone. I've known too many churches whose welcoming pastors were undermined by door-shutting church members. Nevertheless, we need to set an example of openness and encourage it wherever we see it. We need to make our meetings places that are safe enough for people to welcome new ideas, whether they come from the stranger to meeting or from the stranger inside us whose voice needs to be expressed.

I was very privileged for seventeen years to pastor what I lovingly (and with some bias!) call the "best Friends church east of the Mississippi," Williamsburg Friends Meeting, in Indiana. During those years I tried to put into practice the things I've been writing about. Having read this far, you've probably noticed this church community was open before I got there. People felt safe enough in open worship or a Sunday school class to speak about the difficult issues in their lives, even their spiritual doubts. I tried to set wide boundaries inside of which they could explore the implications of the biblical texts I preached. We even ended most sermons with comments, additions, and even sometimes questions and rebuttals from the congregation. And we tried— especially through extending hospitality to mentally and physically disabled folks (and really paying attention to them)—to welcome the voice of the stranger who might be our Teacher. An example from that welcoming place may sum up what education looks like for the Friends pastor.

Early in 2015, I preached a series of sermons at Williamsburg Friends called *Old Stories and Outdated Metaphors*. It was my first attempt at crowd-sourced sermons. I put out the question on social media, "What biblical images are so antiquated that they are impossible to understand today?" I received dozens of responses and chose the most popular ones for my sermons.

Far and away the most difficult image for contemporary Christians and non-Christians to understand is the Adam and Eve and apple story from Genesis chapters one through three. To help the meeting grasp what that old story is about, we listened to short midrashes on the texts from Jewish writers who contributed to David Katz and Peter Lovenheim's book, *Reading Between the Lines: New Stories from the Bible*.[6] Then, trusting that the Spirit who inspired the writers of Genesis was still speaking today, I posed the following question, "If we were to re-imagine the Adam and Eve and apple story for today, what might it sound like?"

The results were astounding. One by one people shared stories of their own "Eden" experiences. They told of very clearly defined moments when they passed from "innocence" to "knowledge." One involved disobeying a parental rule. Another was trespassing and damaging a person's property. In every case, the speaker told of their loss of innocence and how something was gained in that loss. Before the sermon and personal stories were finished, another meeting member spoke. She likened Adam and Eve's expulsion from Eden to how a wood duck pushes its chicks out of the nest when it is time for them to move toward maturity. That interpretation didn't quite match the others, and it didn't jibe with my own theology. However, as I looked around the meeting room, I saw heads nodding. It was as if people were saying, "Oh, *now* I get it."

As Friends pastors—really, as any kind of pastor—we can open the door for people to get it. We don't have to force God's word down people's throats. We can simply create a space—through openness, boundaries, and hospitality—where people can hear the still, small, voice of the Spirit. When we do that, we'll constantly be amazed at how much learning, transformation, and spiritual growth takes place.

# ▪ 8 ▪

## We Just Shake Hands?
## The Friends Pastor and Major Life Events

My wife, Jen, was not brought up Quaker. She was baptized into the Roman Catholic Church, raised Wesleyan, married into (and divorced out of) the Baptist Church, and finally turned away from religion altogether before I ever met her. When we started dating, I was a little hesitant to invite her to church. I was sure the whole "dating a pastor" thing was weird enough for her, and I didn't want to scare her away by asking her to accompany me to church.

Eventually, Jen started coming to meeting for worship and even preached a couple of times. But the event that seemed most strange to her was the Quaker wedding. She read a little about it after we first discussed marriage. At one point she asked, "You mean we don't kiss; we just shake hands?" I tried to explain that kissing was still part of the wedding, but shaking hands concluded the worship service. I think she remained a bit confused until the day we actually wed and she experienced it firsthand.

During my doctoral research, I surveyed pastors and other Quaker leaders about the way Friends handle the rituals that surround significant life events, particularly weddings and funerals. Although some thought my study should not include such things, as they didn't view them differently than pastors of any other denomination might, quite a few survey respondents felt strongly that the way Friends commemorate these events is very closely tied to the beliefs and practices that make Friends unique.

Regarding weddings, one yearly meeting superintendent exclaimed, "We marry none. We witness to relationships that God has joined together. The traditional Friends clearness for marriage in conjunction with a pastor's counsel goes a long way to discern the divine grounding of a proposed marriage."

This brings out the most important feature of the Quaker wedding, one that relates directly to Friends' theological belief that God is present and active in every human endeavor. God does the joining. The church only witnesses communally what God has done in the hearts of the couple whose marriage the meeting celebrates.

A Quaker educator wrote, "I think the historical model of incorporating weddings as part of the worship experience of the church, and the power that comes from the witness of the fellowship (e.g., marriage certificate*) are especially important." And a Friends pastor added, "Friends believe in equality and the ongoing influence of the Holy Spirit, and premarital ministry has to involve preparation of the couple for life under those circumstances, and the wedding needs to be an act of worship according to the Friends understanding of that, too, with the Holy Spirit being in charge of the service."

---

*Here the respondent was referring to the traditional Friends practice of wedding vows being part of a worship service (whether a regularly scheduled Sunday service or a specially called meeting) and everyone in attendance signing a large marriage certificate as a means of corporate witness to the vows and corporate support of the couple.

So how do Friends pastors encourage their meetings in, and support the practice of, the unique and worshipful way Friends celebrate life events? First, we will look more closely at the Quaker way of coming together for two of these events: weddings and funerals. Then I will suggest ways Friends pastors can support their meeting's practices. Finally, we will consider rites of passage common to other Christian groups and how Friends might help their youth negotiate life's landmarks in a healthy, life-affirming manner.

In my "Work of the Pastor" class at Earlham School of Religion, I begin our unit on weddings with a discussion about premarital ministry. The students and I joke a little about the two extreme views on what used to be called "premarital counseling." Those views, at one end of the spectrum, are that premarital ministry is completely useless because no one is listening; and at the other end of the spectrum—we must require a minimum of eight counseling sessions, a complete personality workup, and make every possible attempt to guarantee a strong marriage. While I agree with the intent of the latter and the observation ("no one is listening") of the former, I've found premarital ministry to be a helpful beginning for most couples. I've also found the distinctly Quaker way of providing such ministry particularly useful.

I want to begin with the foundational idea of Friends that marriage should be "under the care of the meeting." This means that the marriage itself, and not just the wedding ceremony, is a community process. When a couple in a Quaker meeting asks to be married under the care of the meeting, they are trying to discern *in community* what is best for their relationship. According to Kate Hood, who worked with others in North Carolina to articulate the process,

The marriage ceremony is the public celebration and solemnization of the union of two people. It brings together family, friends and community to partake in the joy and love of the couple's commitment to each other. In the traditional manner of Friends, the marriage ceremony comes after the couple, together with the Meeting, works through a careful process of clearness.[1]

The way in which the community participates in the marriage process begins with the "clearness committee." Clearness committees are groups (usually four to eight people) chosen by the meeting, or by the couple and the meeting, that meet one or more times with the couple to guide them in thinking about the potential difficulties they might face in their marriage. The committee asks the same kind of questions a premarital survey would ask but does so among people with marriage experience in an atmosphere of mutual support. North Carolina Yearly Meeting's publication, *A Wedding after the Manner of Friends*[2] contains an excellent list of potential questions. (See Appendix.)

When the clearness committee is satisfied that the marriage can be given the support of the meeting, they recommend the couple to the monthly meeting. It is up to the monthly meeting to give final approval to the marriage. After that, a wedding can be scheduled: a simple unprogrammed meeting for worship in which vows are stated, or a more elaborate ceremony.

For persons not familiar with Quaker process, a marriage under the care of the meeting may seem odd or even intrusive. Although I've officiated mostly at weddings that were all but identical to traditional

Protestant ceremonies, two of the weddings that were most personal to me involved variations of the traditional Quaker process: my own and my son's.

Jen's and my wedding process began in a more or less traditional Quaker manner, if by "traditional Quaker" one means subject to the guidance of the Sprit. We asked to be placed under the care of the meeting I was pastoring. We presented a list of names of potential clearness committee members, and this was approved by the meeting. That list included two couples from the congregation who represented two generations and two families; Jen's coworker and best friend, Christi, who was instrumental in Jen and me getting acquainted; and, to clerk the meeting, a former pastor and colleague of mine at ESR who has a lot of experience with clearness committees. It seemed like the perfect mixture of spiritual and marital experience along with love and concern for the couple—us.

With the meeting's approval, we scheduled the clearness committee. On the appointed day and time, Jen and I showed up. The two couples were already at the meetinghouse. Christi arrived shortly after. We all casually chatted, and Jen introduced Christi to the other committee members. Christi grew up in church but more recently could be identified as one of the many "spiritual but not religious" people who populate our landscape. Things like care of the earth, valuing all life, and service toward those in need are far more important to her than one's particular doctrinal views on sin and salvation. A year or so later, I officiated at a very earth-centered wedding ceremony for Christi and her husband. Christi was fascinated with the clearness process, having studied whatever she could find about it on Google.

The time for the meeting came and passed without sight of our committee clerk—the expert we hoped would guide the process. Phone service at the meetinghouse was generally poor, so I wasn't sure if my desperate texts to the clerk were being read. Read or not, no responses came. It was obvious we'd need a new clerk.

Quaker eyes shifted back and forth, waiting for the Spirit to lead someone other than them to clerk the meeting. Finally, Christi said that since she had been studying about clearness committees, she felt she could do the job. Even though she was not a member of the meeting, a Quaker, or even a self-identified Christian, the group sensed a rightness about her clerking. After a time of expectant silence, Christi opened the meeting. As the potential groom, I can give only a very subjective perspective. However, there was a sense of the Spirit moving through us in the way Friends expect the best of clearness committees to work. Committee members later remarked how Spirit-led the meeting seemed.

Since the committee was comprised mostly of married people, a number of the questions were based on real-life situations regarding finances, roles, and conflict. Jen and I felt encouraged but cautioned as the group asked how we would negotiate our twenty-year age difference. Christi expertly led the group by interspersing quiet reflection amid the questions. After every committee member's concerns and encouragement were voiced, she felt free to recommend our proceeding toward marriage.

After receiving the orthodox approval of our unorthodox clearness committee, Jen and I were "found clear to marry" by the monthly meeting. The service, which was held on a Saturday afternoon, included waiting worship, a lot of encouraging messages spoken by attendees, sharing of vows and rings, and both a kiss and a handshake. The absentee clearness committee member officiated and did a wonderful job explaining the Quaker wedding process to the many non-Quakers present. I'm sure our wedding wouldn't satisfy the most Quakerly among us, but I think it was a good example of traditional Friends practice set amid contemporary Midwestern culture.

My son Stephen's wedding exemplifies another kind of marriage under the care of the meeting. At the time he and his fiancée approached the meeting clerk, I was pastoring the meeting he attended. We also had serving with us an intern who was studying at ESR. This man was a good friend of Stephen's, and a person with a few years of pastoral experience. Stephen wanted the intern to officiate at the ceremony, which would blend traditional Protestant with traditional Quaker elements.

Our meeting clerk did not have a lot of experience with clearness committees for marriage, so she exercised a different option for establishing the meeting's care of the couple: she asked the monthly meeting to approve the intern as representing the meeting as a whole. The meeting agreed to abide by the decision of the intern, who would set up a premarital ministry plan, regarding his discernment on the appropriateness of the marriage.

Even though there was no clearness committee in Stephen's wedding process, I believe the meeting acted out of a true sense of care for Stephen and his bride. Rather than abdicating their responsibility, they placed it in the hands of someone they respected and trusted. Members of the monthly meeting felt they were part of the process and joyfully attended the ceremony when it was held some months later.

Because of Friends' openness to the Spirit, these two examples of the wedding process can be considered Quaker, though neither was traditional in a formal sense. I'm sure across the wider body of Friends there are dozens of other variations. It seems to me that amongst most Quakers, the communal nature of weddings, rather than line-by-line adherence to a book of church polity, is the essence of weddings "after the manner of Friends."

The other major life event about which Friends have a distinctive view is the funeral. Once again, in the twenty-first century, most Quaker funerals are somewhat similar to their Protestant counterparts. Still, the way Friends look at funerals is not quite the same as other churches, and it all goes back to that *Presence in the Midst*.

First, there is the expectation that the Holy Spirit will be ministering directly to the grieving family. One yearly meeting superintendent wrote:

> The Friends minister's role in the funeral is helping those gathered sense and recognize the presence of Christ. It is often appropriate for the pastor to do this by leading in prayers, reading scriptures, or voicing messages appropriate for the occasion. At other times the most effective thing the pastor can do is stop talking—so that others may speak and so that Christ's still small voice can be heard. A Friends pastor must be in tune with how the Comforter comes to each family in their grief.

Second, there is the acknowledgement that the funeral is a worship service and not just a ceremony.

Another superintendent wrote, "An unprogrammed Friends memorial meeting for worship can be a powerful witness and celebration of an individual's life." An FUM pastor affirmed, "A funeral is a meeting for worship."

Third, within that meeting for worship there is a time for silence and open worship where speaking may come from anyone in the group assembled. A Friends pastor wrote, "Allowing open worship and the personal remembrances of the deceased seem meaningful to both the involved family and other attenders."

Tom Mullen, writing in *Quaker Life*, contrasted traditional Protestant funerals with Quaker funerals. He said traditional funerals were "handicapped by certain inherent limitations."[3] The limitations Mullen described involved the pastor being at the core of most funerals. And while a pastor who is familiar with the deceased can officiate in a way that truly honors that person and blesses their family, too often the pastor is not familiar with the one whose life is being celebrated. This can produce a rather "canned" funeral service even when the pastor makes every effort to be caring.*

According to Mullen, Friends memorial meetings have a better opportunity to help loved ones through a dark night of their lives. Their essential component—time set aside for silence out of which persons who are led can speak or pray or sing—is a theological reminder

---

*With all respect to Tom Mullen, I have found this often *not* to be the case. Jay Marshall, dean of Earlham School of Religion, conducted a beautiful memorial service for my dad, after meeting for hours with my mom and me. His service was personal and appropriate, truly honoring my father. Actually, the funeral service conducted by Pop's own pastor, after his body was shipped back to Pennsylvania for interment, seemed impersonal and "canned" when compared to Jay's. I guess Tom makes a valid point after all.

that meetings for worship are intended to be led by the Living Christ. But because the silence can be surrounded by other worship forms, music, scripture readings, and prayers can be included that connect to the deceased. Instead of the burden being placed on one person—the pastor—the entire faith community gathers to pool life experiences, love, and insights in an effort to help those who mourn.[4]

For Friends, commemorating a life is a communal experience, like a wedding. Both of these life passages are reflections of the core belief of the presence of God among gathered worshipers. They include invitations to all who are present to speak as they are led by the Spirit. While they often include the leadership of a pastor, there is never an assumption that the pastor is the only one who may minister at the event. These special times are public evidences of the practice of the testimonies* of equality, simplicity, and community.

So what can Friends pastors do to support their meetings during life events like these? I think it goes back to emphasizing the presence of God in our gatherings and reminding our congregants that the Present One inhabits us individually and corporately. We all share in the joy of the wedding, but we also all participate in encouraging and providing spiritual guidance for the couple being married. Perhaps establishing mentorships among experienced wedded members for newlyweds would be a helpful reminder

---

*Quaker "testimonies" are some of the core values of the Society of Friends—beliefs we have been led to over and over by the Spirit—although they have never been written into a creedal statement. The most common contemporary set of testimonies includes simplicity, peace, integrity, community, and equality. Some interpretations of the testimonies add stewardship of the earth.

that "care of the meeting" is more than just a quaint expression. Encouraging intergenerational activities and educational opportunities or making celebrations of *living* meeting members part of our worship services might help the whole meeting feel more of that sense of community when one of our number dies or experiences a loss. As pastors we don't have to provide all the answers to every question, but we can use our knowledge of Friends history and beliefs to help our meetings discover the reasons why we do what we do.

Thinking about the communal nature of life events for Friends made me realize there is a spiritual life event often celebrated in other forms of Christianity, and in other religions, that is largely ignored among Quakers. It is the passage from childhood to adulthood. I remember, growing up in Brooklyn, how excited my Jewish friends were to reach the age when they would become bar/bat mitzvah. The guys I normally played street football with would walk around reciting scripture in Hebrew. They were preparing for the day when, at least spiritually, they would become a man.

Of course, the Irish and Italian kids in my neighborhood also went through spiritual rites of passage at Holy Family Catholic Church or Our Lady of Miracles. They prepared for their confirmation by taking classes to help them understand what it was to be Catholic.

Friends, on the other hand, largely ignore that special time in a young person's life when they realize they are growing up. A young Friend's childhood often begins in a spiritual family—a church or meeting—but as they mature and feel ready for full adult participation in church matters, their readiness can be overlooked. This, I believe, weakens our meetings.

I did not grow up Quaker. I was raised in an independent fundamentalist church that had at one time been part of Methodism. Still, we had our own bylaws and offered church membership to those who requested it and attended some classes. When I was eleven or twelve I remember having a kind of spiritual growth spurt. I wanted to become a greater part of my faith community. I knew my parents and my older brother were members of our church, so I felt it was my time to join. I asked my dad, and he thought it might be a good idea, so he told me to talk to the pastor. The pastor told me I was too young and to wait until I was a teenager to ask about membership. Disappointed, I waited almost until I graduated high school before inquiring about membership again.

I was one of the stubborn ones. I didn't quit church when I was in my teens. I persisted even though I felt I was being ignored. My stubbornness has kept me in the church for a lot of years. Still, would my bond have been stronger if my old pastor had said, "Wow, Phil! I'm glad you're ready to take the next step in your faith journey. Let's celebrate that"?

Celebrating next steps wasn't part of my childhood church. It is not part of many Friends meetings either. Some years ago a student, Philip Raines, turned in his final paper in a religious education class I taught at ESR. He called it *The Friendly Rites* and made a strong case for a Quaker way of celebrating young Friends' spiritual milestones. Raines looked back to early Friends for examples of spiritual milestones. He described the traumatic event when a Quaker received their inner baptism. He also mentioned the eternal and universal communion that happens where Friends gather for worship even without the presence of bread and wine.

To Raines, contemporary Friends practice of meeting membership stems from the old idea of spiritual baptism, but it ignores the "wonderful rebirth that the believer underwent." Believing that young Friends' movement toward spiritual maturity should be celebrated at various stages, he proposed five rites of spiritual passage.[5] These are:

1. The Passage of Silence, which takes seriously Friends commitment to real communion with the living Christ. Raines suggested that children should be trained for participation in worship because it would prepare them for communion. What if we planned for and celebrated a child's participation in worship instead of expecting them to be quiet—which is not the same as silence—or segregating them from adult worship entirely?

2. The Passage of Light. This is Raines' description of spiritual baptism, which he equates with the "struggle to find the Inner Light of Christ within oneself." It is that point in a person's spiritual development at which they own their faith. Raines, contrasting this experience with catechism, says, "Rather than asking children questions about whether or not they believe in a creed, Friends encourage inner exploration and development." This exploration can be assisted by the meeting's educational ministry. It may even involve a sort of vision quest as young Friends are encouraged to find a solitary place where they can reflect on their vision of Christ.

3. The Passage of Membership. Upon completion of their Passage of Light, the child would meet with a clearness committee to determine their readiness for membership in the monthly meeting. This step, according to Raines, "affirms the spiritual journey that has taken place within the child, now a member of the Society."

4. The Passage of Responsibility. Comparing the young Friend to a Jewish boy, who leads the worship service at which he is bar mitzvahed, Raines asks, "Why do we not require new members to both lead and end worship service?" I add, why not make this a rite of passage for all Friends, including—and maybe especially—our young Friends? I wonder how my life would have been different had the pastor I mentioned earlier ushered me into membership with full adult responsibilities rather than telling me to come back when I was older.

5. The Passage of Ministry. This rite celebrates a young Friend's first speaking in waiting worship. Raines says it "signifies a transformation from observer to the call of ministry." It would seem to me to be a logical progress, after one has been trained to listen for the Spirit in worship, and to know when it is appropriate to speak, for the meeting to celebrate when a Friend of any age first engages in vocal ministry.

Something about Raines' ideas has stuck with me over the years. Friends seem so concerned about losing their youth to "the world." And yet, in those places where young Friends are considered to be a vital part of the present meeting—rather than simply being "the future church"—the connection often lasts even when those young people move away from the meeting in which they grew up. It doesn't always work that way, but maybe if we truly welcomed our youth into the full life of the church—in worship and in work and witness—and celebrated that welcome, more of them just might remain committed to the church as they navigate the years of early adulthood.

Celebrations, as we have seen, are an important part of Quaker life and ministry. Even though Friends weddings may look a lot like any other Protestant wedding, and Friends funerals may sometimes resemble others within the local culture, Friends look at these events with different eyes than most of their neighbors. We recognize that special life events are times of worship when the real presence of the living God inhabits and enfolds us. Because of that, the Friends pastor takes a backseat to the Spirit even when that pastor stands in front of the worship room. At these celebrations, we exemplify for our congregations the humbleness that comes from being one among equals, all of whom are residences of the same Spirit.

# ∎ 9 ∎

## It'll Be Okay:
## The Friends Pastor and Pastoral Care

D
ave is not the kind of guy to worry. A full-time farmer, he might get a little concerned when the rains fail to fall regularly during the growing season. He might wonder how many more years he can get out of his old combine and start planning for the huge expense of a new one. But worry? Not Dave. So I was surprised one Sunday when Dave spoke up during the "joys and concerns" part of the worship service* and reported that he would be undergoing cataract surgery that week.

Actually, the surprise was twofold. First, as pastor of a small Friends meeting, I was usually the last to know about things like impending surgery. Folks in smaller churches often rely on each other for pastoral care before bringing the pastor into the mix. Second, Dave didn't seem like the kind of guy whose voice would quiver (a little) over a surgery as common as the procedure for removing a cataract. So I was caught off guard by his genuine request for prayer about the procedure.

While my ministry-experienced and educated mind was considering the best form of pastoral care, Warren, one of the men who lived in a group home, got out of his seat and moved to the pew directly in

---

* I explain this practice in more detail later in this chapter.

front of Dave. Warren turned and faced Dave and said, "I had that surgery two years ago. It'll be okay." If a professional pastor had said that, it would be considered inappropriate. We never say things like, "This happened to me, so...." Most congregants might say that outside of the worship context but would never stop the service to respond to Dave's need. But everything Warren had learned in his years at Quaker meeting told him the right thing to do was to comfort Dave in the most direct way. And why not? Warren was as much a minister as I or any other member of the meeting.

That's the thing about Friends. When we talk about everyone being a minister, we mean it. It's not just a statement in *Faith and Practice*, the Quaker book of church polity. We may not all have the level of training or experience or the same gifts some kinds of ministers have, but we are all led to serve by the same Spirit. Warren seemed to know that, and so he gave unorthodox but perfectly appropriate pastoral care.

Pastoral care, whether through visits to a prison or a healthcare facility, counsel over coffee, or pastoral and prophetic preaching, is a vital part of our job as pulpit ministers. There is nothing intrinsically Quaker about it. Yet in 2001, former Earlham School of Religion professor Bill Ratliff edited a compilation of essays on Quaker views and practices related to pastoral care called *Out of the Silence: Quaker Perspectives on Pastoral Care and Counseling*. "Quaker perspectives" is an interesting way to put it.

Do Friends have a unique way of practicing pastoral care? At least some of the church leaders I interviewed thought so. An Evangelical Friends Church educator wrote,

The Quaker practice of pastoral care and visitation should acknowledge the Friends belief that the Living Christ is ever present as Shepherd and Healer, and those giving pastoral care should embody and communicate the love of Christ. Pastoral counseling in the context of Friends ministry should acknowledge the Quaker concept of the Inner Light, and counseling should be done with the understanding that the resources are within each individual for change and growth.

And in keeping with Friends belief that every believer is a minister, an Evangelical Friends yearly meeting superintendent wrote regarding whether there is a uniquely Quaker way of doing pastoral care and visitation, "Yes, I think so, but maybe mostly in terms of how we help the community be involved in this ministry. That is, we can create an environment in which the broader church—the elders, others with pastoral gifts, etc.—work alongside the pastor to carry out this vital ministry."

It would appear that basic pastoral caregiving could fall under the banner of ministry performed in a uniquely Quaker manner. While I believe that many pastors of every faith desire to be led by God in their ministry of care, it would seem, at least to some of my respondents, that Friends look more intently for this to happen. The question then becomes, how? How do Friends model this Spirit-led expectancy in pastoral care?

In her chapter in *Out of the Silence*, pastoral counselor Maureen Graham identifies three ways in which Friends engage in pastoral care. They closely parallel the way I have given and received such care in my thirty-plus years ministering among Friends. The first characteristic of Quaker pastoral care is sacrament: Friends do pastoral care *sacramentally*.

Sacraments are, according to St. Augustine, "outward signs of inward grace."[1] In a very real sense, they are encounters with the God of grace. For Friends, this is what happens in the meeting for worship as described in an earlier chapter. However, since Jesus said that wherever two or three gather in His name, He is there (Matthew 18:20), one could say that every pastoral care encounter is a meeting for worship—an event where the living Christ is present and active. Friends believe that. In pastoral care, according to Friends, the Spirit communes directly with both the care giver and the care receiver in ways that draw them both toward a center neither may have expected.

Sometimes this encounter is one-to-one, like the moment that occurred when Warren and Dave and Jesus met in the story that began this chapter. That was a sacramental moment of pastoral care. Everyone who witnessed Warren's motion of love toward Dave knew God was intimately present. Sometimes, however, sacramental pastoral care affects an entire group.

Most Friends meetings, whether programmed or unprogrammed, include a time of personal sharing called "Joys and Concerns," or some such name. This is not a form of waiting or open worship. During Joys and Concerns, people are not waiting for a leading from the Spirit; rather, they are bringing before the meeting something that is on their heart at that moment. It could be a request for prayer for a neighbor, relative, or themselves. It could be a way to make public some good news they recently received.

Joys and Concerns time can be an expression of sacramental pastoral care that envelops the entire assembled meeting, or it can be a weekly litany of ailments with the weak promise to remember that person in prayer. Often, it is the pastor or worship leader who makes the difference. The one who presides over these crucial moments has the wonderful responsibility of welcoming the divine Presence into those moments and making them holy.

During my tenure as pastor at Williamsburg Friends Meeting, we would end our worship service with Joys and Concerns followed by a prayer in which everyone present would get out of their seats and hold hands. I'd call it a prayer circle, but it was never really a circle. Depending on attendance it could be oblong, L-shaped, or T-shaped. The phrase "prayer amoeba" might be more descriptive. Often there were persons present who were unable to stand easily, so the amoeba engulfed them, holding hands all the while.

The Williamsburg prayers offered all kinds of sacramental care. Sometimes I would pray as the pastor, and sometimes it felt right for the prayer to come from someone else. More than a few times the folks from the group homes would offer verbal prayers along with—and sometimes alongside—the pastor. I remember times when the leaders of that meeting for worship would place their hands on a person who either had requested prayer for themselves or could stand in for someone needing prayer. These instances were by their very nature sacraments because they focused the grace of God on the community of God's people. True, there were times it only felt like we were ending the service. More often than not, however, we left the meeting with a sense of the Presence of God having been with us. The simple act of giving pastoral care through prayers and touch and encouragement drew us to a divine Center.

According to Graham, the second characteristic of pastoral care among Friends is relationality: Friends do pastoral care *relationally*. Mutuality exists between care giver and care receiver. This is a place in ministry where the minister, be they pastor or otherwise, can lead and also be led, receive as well as give. Graham writes, "As pastoral care givers, we are called to risk entering more honestly and more compassionately into relationship and dialogue with others."[2]

The idea of a pastor receiving care in the process of giving reminds me of Jesus' words to Peter. There beside the lake, after a hearty breakfast, Jesus and Peter have their "do you love me" conversation. Then Jesus adds, "Very truly, I tell you, when you were younger, you used to fasten your own belt and go wherever you wished. But when you grow old, you will stretch out your hands, and someone else will fasten a belt around you and take you where you do not wish to go" (John 21:18 NRSV). John describes Jesus' words as a prophecy of Peter's future martyrdom. To me it's more a matter of vulnerability. There will come a time in Peter's life when he can no longer be the master of his fate. He will have to submit to being led even when he has no choice in the matter. This is the ultimate vulnerability.

While I hope none of us will be led to martyrdom, I know that if we are truly offering relational pastoral care, there will be times when our vulnerability results in our being led even as we assume our place of leadership.

This idea of mutuality in pastoral care became very personal to me when I visited a parishioner on a day where I'd rather have been anywhere else. Family matters were weighing heavy on my heart. There were difficult decisions to be made, and I just didn't know how to make them. Meanwhile, I had to visit Rachel.

Rachel's diabetes had taken her in and out of hospitals for many years. For as long as I'd known her, every hospital visit had resulted in the removal of one more piece of her frail body: a foot, a leg, the other foot, the other leg. I wondered how much more could be taken from her. More than that, I wondered what I could offer Rachel by way of comfort. Not being gifted in pastoral caregiving anyway, and seeing Rachel disappear before my eyes year after year, I reluctantly pulled my car into a space at the rehab center where she was undergoing post-operative therapy. I didn't feel like talking to anyone, and certainly felt in no shape to offer care to someone in Rachel's circumstances.

I walked into Rachel's room and began making small talk, sports I think. Rachel was a football fan. Time passed more quickly than I expected, but, eventually, I felt I needed to say something supportive and "pastoral." Rachel didn't give me the chance. Looking directly into my eyes from her bed, she said, "May I pray for you?" She'd seen through my façade all along. The light conversation, my attempt at being a caregiver, they could not hide the struggle in my heart. With tears welling up in my eyes I said, "Please do."

After Rachel's prayer and a little more light conversation, I got ready to leave. "Rachel," I said, "Why do I always leave here as the one being ministered to instead of the minister?" She had no answer. We both knew it was because in that room there were two ministers. Which one happened to be offering care on any given day was simply a matter of need and action.

The third way Friends do pastoral care is *prophetically*. We cannot address the pain without considering the causes of that pain. Graham writes, "In line with our Quaker tradition, we are called to speak and act without violence as witnesses to the truth that we see and hear. We are called to respond to the relational woundedness of our world and to engage the task of healing broken hearts, souls, bodies, and relationships."[3]

One of the primary ways in which Friends combine pastoral care and prophetic ministry is in preaching. The relationship between pastoral care and prophetic preaching is symbiotic. We cannot truly care for a congregation without being willing to challenge them to stand against anything that would threaten the vision of God's reign in the world. At the same time, we earn the right to issue such a challenge through the strength of our pastoral relationship with the congregation, and pastoral preaching is one way that happens.

I recall a conversation with Bill, my right-hand person—literally, he sat in the pulpit chair to my right—song leader, and number-one heckler. He surprised me by saying that he didn't like me at first, and he didn't think much of my sermons. However, he admitted, after years of my demonstrating my care for his family, I sort of grew on him. In later years, I was able to speak with much more power on controversial issues, at least in Bill's presence, because he knew I had his family's best interests at heart.

As pastors, we also have the opportunity to offer prophetic pastoral care to the wider community in which we live. Friends pastor Leigh Tolton tells of a time when she was working with a United Church of Christ congregation in the heart of a southern city.

From her office window, she could watch the parade of sex workers on the way to their street corners. Tolton began taking her breaks at a time and place where she could engage the women in conversation.

Quite a few of the women wanted to talk. They shared stories of their lives and their children, their hopes, fears, and dreams. Tolton listened and offered what pastoral care they seemed to need. The church included the women's children in fun activities at Halloween and Easter.

Eventually a local pimp got concerned about his employees spending time with a pastor, and he wanted to put a stop to it. Although he tried to intimidate Tolton by yelling, she knew it was time to take pastoral care to the next level. She spoke quietly to the man and offered to make a deal with him. "How long do these girls work for you before they're worn out and can't make any more money for you?" Tolton asked.

Intrigued, the man replied, "A year, two most of the time if they're young enough."

Tolton pressed her case, "What if they signed up for their GEDs while they could, would you let them do that?" Tolton told him how it would increase their self-esteem, attract better clientele, and when he was finished with them they would have hope for other work.

"And not think it's my fault I can't use them, right? Don't let this education go to their heads, though," he said with a warning.

Tolton later learned that six of the young women eventually signed up for GED classes. By coupling pastoral care with long-term action, this Quaker pastor was able to make a lasting impact. We offer pastoral care prophetically when we address not just the immediate need of a person but when we also address the injustice and other causes that led to the need.

To Maureen Graham's description of Quaker pastoral care I would add a fourth quality: *kairos*. According to the Merriam-Webster online dictionary, "kairos" refers to an "opportune and decisive moment."[4] Friends do pastoral care *kairotically*—in the moment. We do not plan out every pastoral care experience, as if by planning we can somehow bring healing, wisdom, or resolution to a situation. Rather we look for opportunities to arise where the Spirit seems to be moving, and then we try our best to follow. But again, we as pastors are only one small part of the process. Every member and attender can also be part of it.

Sometimes those opportunities occur without warning right in the meeting for worship. I remember a Sunday morning when I preached a sermon that spoke to me in a way I didn't anticipate. At the end I gave a rare altar call, and then I was the first one on my knees at the rail. As I prayed, conversing with God about whatever it was that was so heavy on my heart, I felt a hand on my shoulder. The pressure was light but firm. I felt a warmth emanating from that touch. Eventually, my burden was released. I opened my eyes and began to stand. There behind me stood Dave, the farmer whose story introduced this chapter. He lifted his big hand from my shoulder and hugged me. In that moment, with Dave as pastoral caregiver and me as care-receiving pastor, everything that is reflected in the phrase "Quaker pastoral ministry" came together.

To pastor in the moment is to be constantly open to the Spirit's leading. This sounds impossible and sometimes feels that way as well. But we keep trying. We are not willing to embrace the status quo. We know that in the next meeting, perhaps even in the next minute of *this* meeting, there will rise up a Warren to minister to Dave and a Dave to minister to us.

You know, we're a fortunate bunch, we pastors. We get to be with people during their most joyous times and their most vulnerable moments. At the same time, we experience joy, and we can be vulnerable ourselves. Our job is to offer pastoral care, to model pastoral care, to encourage those in our meetings to become caregivers according to their gifts, and, at times, to receive pastoral care from those we are called to serve. If you feel like saying, "Wow!" about now, I will join you.

# • 10 •

## Starting Over—Again:
## The Friends Pastor and The Future

This morning I am sitting in church. There's a grill on the northwest corner where Jaimie is frying bacon and turning eggs over-easy. Guys in Harley-Davidson t-shirts are drinking coffee at the counter. A woman rushes in to pick up her family's breakfast order.

You're right. It's a restaurant, my favorite hole-in-the wall in Richmond, Indiana. (Come visit and I'll take you there for biscuits and gravy.) The owners staked everything they owned or could borrow to buy the place. They know success depends not just on good cooking but good customer service. The clientele knows this café to be a place where honest conversation can take place at and between tables and counter stools. This is the church. These are the people among whom Christ dwells. How will Friends pastors serve and lead this church-that's-everywhere as it moves through the twenty-first century?

I've been asking myself that question a lot over the years that I've taught pastoral ministry at Earlham School of Religion. I knew the church was in transition when I arrived at my office in July of 1999. I've seen it changing faster and faster. My goal now, as retirement looms on the horizon, is to ride that change and adjust my classes to meet the needs of a new church.

Just what *are* the needs of that church? I don't profess to know all of them, or even to understand how church will be church during the rest of this century. I know of trends in North American culture that seem to be leading toward some very fruitful possibilities for Quaker ministry, and I believe that Quakers are uniquely qualified to meet the spiritual needs of people today.

The world of faith has changed remarkably during my lifetime, and much of it was brought about by, or in response to, my generation, the Baby Boomers. We created a major shift in the greater culture and society—and nowhere more strongly than in the religious character and church structures of North America. One example was our effect on church music. Tired of traditional hymns and gospel songs, we created something called "contemporary Christian music," which the next generation distilled into not-so-catchy choruses.

Boomers changed the focus of church architecture as well. We hardly ever spoke to our neighbors in the suburbs, but we wanted to enjoy fellowship with other church folk, so we made sure church buildings include larger lobbies than the older generation's vestibules, and then we filled them with coffee kiosks to fuel our pre-service gatherings.

We spent our young adult years bouncing from church to church, looking for our needs to be met by clean, safe church nurseries and lots of activities. And something about these changes—symptoms of a greater social change—led to our children walking away from the church in droves. *Their* children seem to be quitting religion itself and barely giving God the benefit of the doubt. Maybe the church of our parents, of ours, and of our children's is no longer relevant to today's society. Do we need to close the shop called church? Last one out, please turn off the lights and lock the doors.

Okay, that's a rather dismal point of view, but you know what? Trying to rescue a dying church is something Quakers learned not to do a long time ago. The first Friends—George Fox, Margaret Fell, James Naylor, that bunch—didn't try to save the church. In their view the Anglican Church was corrupt, and Christians everywhere just weren't getting it. What did they do?

After speaking their truth within the churches of their time—and facing persecution for it—they created a new kind of religion. Or, rather, they revived what they thought to be Christianity in its earliest, most essential, form. They stripped Christianity of everything they felt had been added over the years: stripped it down to awareness of God's presence, listening to the voice of Spirit, and doing the gospel, the essence of which is loving God and loving people. Without requiring fancy buildings, they were a mobile group who could practice their version of faith literally anywhere two or three were gathered. To this day, most Friends meetinghouses reflect that early simplicity of design. But architecture is not where the first Friends stood out in their time. Rather, it was their core value of God with us—all of us—without even a "them." That is the heart of Quaker ecclesiology, as I've asserted previously, and I believe it will create many new opportunities for ministry, some of it pastoral, in the near future.

Way back in 1993, Wade Clark Roof began observing how North Americans desired to experience what he called "firsthand religion." In words both descriptive and critical, he writes,

The concern is to experience life directly, to have an encounter with God or the divine, or simply with nature and other people, without the intervention of inherited beliefs, ideas, and concepts. Such striving is understandable, not simply because secondhand religion can be empty of meaning, but because only personal experience is in some sense authentic and empowering. Individuals are inclined to regard their own experiences as superior to the accounts of others, and the truths found through self-discovery as having greater relevance to them than those handed down by way of creed or custom. Direct experience is always more trustworthy, if for no other reason than because of its "inwardness" and "within-ness"—two qualities that have come to be much appreciated in a highly expressive, narcissistic culture.[1]

Since then, a lot of folks have critiqued the narcissistic culture of Baby Boomers, Gen-Xers, and now, Millennials. But in all the criticism we forget the observation that people take their own experiences more seriously than they take words on paper, tablet, or phone. Quakers have always known this. As much as they loved the Bible, "what canst *thou* say" supplemented it. They believed the Spirit who authored the Bible was alive and well and still speaking to and through people, so experiential knowledge of the divine rose to the top of their theology.

Friends pastors who have seen God at work in the kinds of experiences I've described in the preceding pages can ride the crest of this cultural wave by validating the experiences shared by members of their meetings. We can teach people to reflect theologically on the everyday aspects of their lives: work, play, family. We can help folks see that of God in people and nature around them. They are *looking* for God, I truly believe. We can help them see.

Sociologists describe the largest single North American belief group today as "spiritual but not religious." Religious pollsters label them "nones," as in "none of the above." They want the spiritual. They need community. And here, for the better part of four centuries, sits an entire denomination quietly seeking communion with a spiritual reality they can experience firsthand. If the spirit of this present moment is experiential spirituality, how is the current state of Quaker, or any other pastoral ministry, suited to it? I believe two trends in which Friends pastors are playing an active role—bivocational pastorates and entrepreneurial ministry—are at least some of the keys whereby the church as a whole can positively affect the lives of those within and those outside its walls.

*In Trust*, the magazine published by the In Trust Center for Theological Schools, recently reported that "the number of dual-career ministers continues to rise." It goes on to cite statistics that show almost fifty percent of current Mennonite pastors are bivocational.[2] Not long ago, I had a conversation with Dennis Bickers, author of numerous books on bivocational ministry. Bickers mentioned that bivocational pastorates are nearing the fifty percent rate even among Southern Baptists, the largest Protestant denomination in the USA.[3] Bivocational ministry is a reality for many, if not most, North American pastors.

However, bivocational ministry has always been part of the church. The apostle Paul supported his missionary work by occasionally hanging out the tentmaking shingle that signified his trade, his "other job." Circuit-riding Methodist preachers returned to their farms on Sunday night. Lately however, with the decline in traditional church attendance that has affected virtually every Christian denomination, the ideal of a fully-funded* pastorate is becoming a dream for seminary graduates. Personally, I have supplemented a less-than-fully-funded pastorate by delivering pizzas, clerking in a hardware store, and substitute teaching. I've also coupled a career as a seminary professor with pastoral ministry among Friends who cannot afford even a half-time preacher. I know, believe in, teach, and live bivocational ministry.

Pastors and congregants have many reasons for embracing bivocational ministry. Congregations generally point first to the financial blessing of not having to pay a full-time salary. Some, however, appreciate the way having a part-time pastor forces them to do the kind of ministry in the church that has traditionally been reserved for the full-time pastor or other paid staff. Isn't that what the Quaker (and other denominations) concept of the ministry of every believer is all about?

Pastors have their own reasons for enjoying bivocational ministry. A few years ago, I traveled from Pennsylvania to Oregon, surveying bivocational pastors and members of their congregations. Just prior to my trip, I tested a few survey questions with the assistant manager at my local Tim Horton's coffee shop. He also serves part-time as a rabbi on staff at a Dayton

*Credit for this phrase goes to Dennis Bickers.

synagogue. He said he loves the connection working at Tim Horton's gives him with real people in real settings. Christian pastors echo that sentiment almost every time I bring up the subject.

Bivocational pastors relish the many opportunities they have to minister to people while at their other job. An Iowa pastor works almost full-time at a bowling alley. He finds two things quite fulfilling in his job. First, as someone who likes to see jobs through to completion—a luxury pastors don't often get—he enjoys being able to hear the call that a lane has malfunctioned, dispatch a repair person, and know within minutes that the crisis is resolved, and the bowlers are bowling again. Second are those quieter moments when he can help fit a person for their first bowling shoes and listen to their story. He wishes the church and bowling alley weren't so far apart geographically because he thinks a lot of people he has gotten to know from the alley would love to attend his church. But even if they can't get to his church, or don't want to attend any church, this man is their pastor. He connects to his customers at a spiritual level, and they appreciate that.

The key to ministry "in the world" is taking seriously people's current state of spiritual development exactly as is it, without judgment and without prefabricated prescriptions. Any time a minister, be they a paid pastor or a co-worker, can create this type of relationship with someone, they have the perfect opportunity to follow George Fox's admonition of "answering that of God in everyone."

It really doesn't take much effort to get people talking about spiritual things these days. I've had some wonderful conversations with strangers who noticed I was reading at the local pub or coffee shop, and they asked what book it was. Books by Paulo Coelho, Peter Rollins, and Diana Butler Bass have led to some deep spiritual sharing. Not long ago, I was in a restaurant reading molecular biologist Kenneth Miller's *Finding Darwin's God*. The server was so intrigued with the idea of a scientist believing in God *because of*, rather than *in spite of*, evolution that I loaned the book to her. I lose more books that way, and I love it. Because bivocational ministers seem to spend more of their time where the people are, they are in a prime position to meet and engage in spiritual conversation with "nones" or anyone else.

There is, however, a caveat when doing ministry in connection with one's job. In my bivocational ministry class at Earlham School of Religion, I warn students against actively seeking ministry opportunities in their secular work. No one wants to be "buttonholed for Christ" on the job, and employers really frown on that. However, I also tell them that opportunities come up all the time, and they will have plenty of space to minister in appropriate ways—from a prayer while on break to a scheduled counseling appointment off company time.

My first bivocational ministry job was when I pastored a Friends meeting in Ohio at about a half-time salary with benefits. I delivered pizza for a Domino's down the street from the meetinghouse. After the initial feelings of discomfort at having a minister on site three nights a week wore off, the staff accepted me as one of their own and even resumed the kind of language they'd worked hard at stifling at first. I learned a lot from them—not the language; I already knew those words. I learned about pastoring a church that doesn't go to church. Bivocational pastors do that. They pastor in ways that don't fit neatly into the reports they must fill out for their denominational leadership. You can't count butts in seats when there are no seats. But that's often where ministry happens. In bivocational ministry there are times when traditional church happens in nontraditional ways.

Some months after I started working at Domino's, my store manager said, "Phil, it's not like I have anything against the church, it's just that churches aren't open when I can go. I work 'til 4:00 a.m. every Saturday night, and I have to be there to open the store at 4:00 on Sunday afternoon. If there was a church open at 4:30 in the morning I'd be there, and I bet the other store managers would be there too." There were three Domino's stores in that city at the time, each with two assistant managers. So I said, "All right, starting next Sunday we'll have church at 4:30 in the morning. The lights'll be on, and the doors'll be open. I'll remind you Saturday night." For the next year and a half, I met with anywhere from two to ten Domino's employees at 4:30 every Sunday morning for a Bible study based on the sermon I would preach later in the morning. One assistant manager's wife and kids started coming to Sunday school and the regular morning worship. It was wonderful when, the next summer at our church picnic, the men and women from Domino's showed up before going to work that Sunday afternoon. Our two congregations had joint fellowship for the first time.

That Domino's store created another kind of bivocational ministry opportunity, one I truly could not have had unless I was a pizza guy. It concerned a coworker named Gary. Gary's wife and daughters went to church somewhere, but Gary didn't. He was happily non-religious. I never really thought that a non-religious person could be happy until I met Gary.

Maybe my understanding of "that of God in everyone" began with him.

One winter night, Gary was out with friends and they dropped him off in the alley behind his house. They didn't notice Gary had slipped on the ice and slid under the car. The car dragged him about one hundred feet down the alley before they stopped. Gary, already a kidney transplant recipient, was in terrible shape. He was in the intensive care unit for many weeks, on a respirator three separate times for multiple days each time. Only his family could see him, although people from Domino's wanted to know how he was doing. Since I was a pastor, I was able to visit him, which I did almost every day.

At first, all I could do was sit in his room and tell him about work, even when he was unconscious. Later, he was conscious but could not talk. So I continued to keep him informed about Domino's and the Cincinnati Reds, his favorite team. Eventually, Gary was able to speak again. One of the first things he told his wife was, if he ever got out of the hospital, they were going to go to my church as a family.

When Gary was finally able to go home, he needed lots of physical therapy. One form of therapy was his getting back into dart playing. But he needed someone to collect his darts until he could walk again. I'd go over to his house a few afternoons a week and do that. He taught me how to play darts. We talked for hours each week over my trips back and forth to the board. Imagine a fully-funded pastor trying to fit that into her busy week.

When he was able, Gary made good on his word to his wife. The family started attending the church. Gary and I wound up starting a men's fellowship group on Friday nights centering on, of all things, darts (in a Quaker meetinghouse!). He donated a beautiful bristle dart board that hung in the fellowship hall for years. The first Christmas Gary was in church, we had our annual Christmas program on a Sunday night. His kids were in it, as were mine. Gary arrived early that night, and I asked him if he'd light the candles in the windows, knowing he smoked and would have a lighter. He did, and that's all the thought I gave it.

Gary's family attended meeting every Sunday for as long as I remained there and for a while after. A few years later, Gary's sister called me and told me he'd died. His body never fully recovered from the accident and from the complications it caused in his other conditions. They asked if I'd do his funeral, and I flew back from Oregon for it. After the funeral service, Gary's mother and sister came over to talk to me. They said that although Gary would never have said anything about it, his entire life changed after that Christmas service. Lighting those candles seemed to give him a purpose in life he'd never had before. I wonder what might have happened to Gary if there wasn't a bivocational pastor in his pizza place.

The fact that bivocational ministry often places pastors where the people are—especially the people who may be spiritual but not religious, or maybe not even spiritual—gives them a chance to know firsthand the ones among whom ministry must happen for the church to grow and thrive. The bivocational minister, who is also a Quaker, is perfectly suited to the flexibility of ministering outside of the box we call church. Who else would expect to find "that of God" living and working in bowling alleys and pizza places?

Before leaving bivocational ministry, I want to point out another ministry possibility when the pastor works a second job. When I was in seminary we had to do a year of what was known as "field education," now often called "supervised ministry." It consists of ministry in a specific field setting or with a particular project, and it is supplemented by a weekly meeting with a mentor who helps the student reflect theologically on an incident from their week. Students often wish they could continue such a relationship after they graduate. I encourage my advisees to find a person with whom they can reflect on their ministry on a regular basis.

But what about bivocational ministers? They have two or more ministries. With whom do they reflect on their teaching job, their pizza delivery service, their ministry of bus driving? This hit home with me very recently when, due to a short-term financial need, I started working fifteen hours a week at a local big box store in addition to my full-time teaching. Things were happening at my new job that I needed to process with someone who might understand their theological and ministry implications.

A few months ago I contacted a bivocational pastor friend, a United Methodist. I asked if we might meet, maybe every two weeks or once a month, to talk about things that happen at work. It could be something of major importance, a personal issue, or an almost insignificant event that might have more value when reflected upon. We agreed to use the weekly reflection tool ESR's Supervised Ministry class uses for theological reflection between intern and supervisor. The first meeting went well, and although our social work and department store calendars don't synchronize as much as we'd like, we've been able to meet at least once every three weeks. The reflections on work events have given us even greater appreciation of the God who is present outside of the church building.

My wife, Jen, joins us at these theological reflection sessions. She believes what we are doing is *church*, not just pastoral work. She would like to see this kind of theological reflection incorporated in every church service so people like her, who work in offices and factories, can do the same kind of deep reflection on God's activity in their everyday lives. I believe she makes a strong point. Why should church be only a one-way conversation from pastor to pew? Whether the context is Quaker or Methodist or none of the above, shouldn't congregations be encouraged to reflect on God's immediate presence with them at work, at home, wherever, and to talk about those reflections with like-minded people? Perhaps bivocational pastors, with their feet in the world, can understand this better than fully-funded pastors. Maybe they can find a way, even in the worship setting, to bridge the gap between secular and sacred because they walk that bridge every day.

Some ministers, Quaker and otherwise, are moving out even farther, and this is where the second trend—entrepreneurial ministry—comes into play. As I write this, the first cohort of students in Earlham School of Religion's graduate Certificate in Entrepreneurial Ministry is completing their final class. The Certificate, while not necessarily related to a degree (although two members of the cohort are using some of the courses toward their Master of Divinity degree), is awarded to recognize completion of six classes of concentrated study and practice related to creating and funding new ministries outside the walls of the local church. All are Friends, although future cohorts may be open to any seminary graduate with a vision for new ministry in the marketplace. These ministers are not opposed to the traditional church format, but they believe that is only one part of the church.

The ministers in the first cohort learned tools for creating a business plan; strategies for obtaining, earning, and using money in a way consistent with Christian ethics and Quaker integrity; and methods of building up the spiritual support needed to sustain the entrepreneur beyond the adrenalin–stoked start-up. During the eighteen months of planning and testing, one student expanded her advanced yoga training to include an online "yoga church," complete with Christ-centered messages and spiritual community. Another student launched a coffee shop in Colombia that caters to the cycling crowd and empowers both the women of the community and internationally-ranked female cyclists. Several Kenyan students are starting farming-based businesses/ministries in Kenya and Rwanda that will provide a model leading to greater self-sufficiency for East African families. And that's only about half the cohort.

My connection to the group was as the instructor for a class called Models of Alternative Ministry. The aim of the class was to acquaint these innovators with some of the many thousands of ways the church is living out its mission in the world. Through the course we met men and women who traded youth ministry for hairstyling because they felt they could make a greater impact in their community through opening a hair salon. We learned about a Friends pastor who focuses his ministry on grief care for children and youth, providing all-expenses-paid retreats funded by his horse boarding business. We even interviewed the owners of the restaurant with whom this chapter began. They're not a religious couple, but I believe their welcoming atmosphere and excellent customer service has something to teach seminary students. That's why I occasionally have my classes meet there. Who knows? Tomorrow's church might meet in places just like that.

Where are Quaker pastors in relation to these innovative forms of ministry? I believe they belong right in the thick of it. We call what buildings we have *meetinghouses*. They're just places where we get together. But people get together in pubs and coffee shops and libraries and town halls and parks and... well, you get the idea. The church—the *ekklesia*—is called together for a reason, and then they disperse into the world to do the real work of loving neighbors and enemies, serving others, and making disciples for a kingdom already at work in the world. No group of people is better suited to this than the ones who are already waiting expectantly for God to burst into a meeting, sit beside them on a bus, provide clarity for a decision, teach them directly, and throw the occasional monkey wrench into their best-laid plans—the Friends pastor, and maybe even you.

# APPENDIX

## Queries for Those Considering Marriage
*Queries* from New Garden Friends Meeting,
North Carolina Fellowship of Friends
(Friends United Meeting)[1]

### Clearness Commmittee

Guided by the Queries for Marriage, it is the task of the clearness committee to labor carefully with the couple and to explore the spiritual, emotional and physical basis of their intended commitment. The committee should help the couple clarify their relationship and counsel them on whatever tensions and problems might arise.

### Queries

- What are your notions of spirituality? In what way do you see your intended marriage as the reflection of your spiritual commitments to each other? How do you plan to bring spirituality into your relationship and through that into the world at large?

- How would each of you describe what you hope for and expect from your marriage relationship? What reservations do you have about marriage? Have you shared these matters with your partner?

■ How openly and clearly can you communicate with each other? What process do you go through in making decisions? How are you able to handle anger and conflict?

■ What are your feelings about privacy, freedom and trust? What experiences do you have, either from your own family or from previous relationships that might affect your marriage? Have you discussed these with your partner?

■ What do you feel is the basis of your friendship with each other? What activities do you share? Are you comfortable with each other's needs for friendship outside the relationship?

■ What duties and responsibilities to each other will you undertake in the establishment of a home? What additional responsibilities and commitments will compete for your time?

■ What role do you expect your families of origin to play in your lives? How will you share holidays with extended family?

■ What are your similarities and differences with regard to managing your lives? Do you organize your time and your belongings in similar ways? If not, have you discovered ways to work around the differences?

■ What plans do each of you have for employment? How do you plan to manage the finances of the home? What are your attitudes about money?

■ Have you clarified your feelings about the possibility of children? What are your attitudes about family planning? If you desire children, do you have similar attitudes about raising them? Would you be happy without children? How do you feel about adoption?

■ Do you expect to be comfortable regarding the role of sexuality in your marriage? Do you share the same opinion about the value of fidelity in your relationship?

■ Are you aware of any medical problems that might influence your marriage and your future?

■ If the marriage is in any way unconventional, how do you intend to meet any obstacles that may result? What are the feelings of your family and friends?

■ What problems do you believe might be serious enough to lead you to divorce?

# ENDNOTES

## Chapter 1

1.  John L. Nickalls, *Journal of George Fox*. (Philadelphia: Religious Society of Friends), 1.

2.  Ibid., 11.

3.  Ibid., 107.

4.  D. Elton Trueblood, *The People Called Quakers.* (Richmond, IN: Friends United Press, 1971), 107.

5.  William Edmundson, *A journal of the life, travels, sufferings, and labour of love in the work of the ministry, of that worthy elder and faithful servant of Jesus Christ, William Edmundson.* (Dublin: Christopher Bentham, 1820), under "Section VI."

6.  Hugh Barbour and J. William Frost, *The Quakers.* (Richmond, IN: Friends United Press, 1988), 39.

7.  Thomas D. Hamm, *The Transformation of American Quakerism: Orthodox Friends, 1800-1907.* (Bloomington, IN: Indiana University Press, 1988), 8.

8.  Ibid.

9.  Samuel Bownas, *A description of the qualifications necessary to a gospel minister.* (Philadelphia: Pendle Hill Publications, 1989), 3.

10. Ibid., 13.

11. Nickalls, *Journal of George Fox*, 7.

12. Hamm, *Transformation of American Quakerism*, 92.

13. Ibid., 125.

14. Ibid.

15. Hamm, *Transformation of American Quakerism*, 126.

16. See Judith Boulbie, *A testimony for truth against all hireling-priests and deceivers.... Also a testimony against all observers of times and dayes.* 1665. Electronic Publisher: Earlham School of Religion: Digital Quaker Collection. Book # E27658342. Accessed January 21, 2009.

17. Hamm, *Transformation of American Quakerism*, 127.

18. Joel Bean, "The pastoral movement." *The British Friend* 47, No. 1 (January), 1889.

19. Hamm, *Transformation of American Quakerism*, 128.

## Chapter 2

1. Howard Brinton, *Friends for 300 Years*. (New York: Harper and Brothers, 1952), 59.

2. Veli-Matti Kärkkäinen, *An Introduction to Ecclesiology: Ecumenical, Historical & Global Perspectives*. (Downers Grove, IL: InterVarsity, 2002), 62, 65.

3. Nickalls, *Journal of George Fox*, 107.

4. Trueblood, *The People Called Quakers*. (Richmond, IN: Friends United Press, 1971), 88.

5. Ibid.

6. Brinton, *Friends for 300 Years*, 84.

7. Stan Thornburg, "Open worship." *Quaker Life*, Series 38, No. 6 (1997), 20-21.

8. Wilmer A. Cooper, *A Living Faith: An Historical Study of Quaker Beliefs*. (Richmond, IN: Friends United Press, 1970), 85.

9. Ibid.

10. Lloyd Lee Wilson, *Essays on the Quaker Vision of Gospel Order*. (Philadelphia: Friends General Conference, 2001), 133-134.

11. Cooper, *A Living Faith*, 8.

12. Jack L. Willcuts, *Why Friends Are Friends*. (Newberg, OR: Barclay Press, 1984), 76.

13. Thomas D. Hamm, *The Quakers in America*. (New York: Columbia University Press, 2003), 34.

14. Ira V. Brown, "Pennsylvania's Antislavery Pioneers, 1688-1776." *Pennsylvania History: A Journal of Mid-Atlantic Studies*, Vol. 55, No. 2 (1988), 64-65.

15. Ibid., 65.

16. Ibid., 73.

17. Richard P. Ratliff, *Our Special Heritage: The Sesquicentennial Publication of Indiana Yearly Meeting of Friends*. (New Castle, IN: Community Printing Co., 1970), 69.

18. Dean Freiday, *Barclay's Apology in Modern English*. (Newberg, OR: Barclay Press, 1991), 85.

19. Nickalls, *Journal of George Fox*, 263.

20. Brinton, *Friends for 300 Years*, 159.

21. Cooper, *A Living Faith*, 137.

22. Brinton, *Friends for 300 Years*, 177.

## Chapter 4

1. Henri J.M. Nouwen, *In the Name of Jesus: Reflections on Christian Leadership* (New York: Crossroad, 1996), 78-81.

## Chapter 5

1. Nickalls, *Journal of George Fox*, 263.

2. Written by David Strasser and Richard Mullins. Copyright © Universal Music Publishing Group, Capitol Christian Music Group.

## Chapter 6

1. Stephen W. Angell and Pink Dandelion. *The Oxford Handbook of Quaker Studies*. (Oxford: Oxford University Press, 2013), 256.

2. Translated by Beltza Jimenez.

## Chapter 7

1. Nickalls, *Journal of George Fox*,107.

2. Parker J. Palmer, *To Know as We Are Known: Education as a Spiritual Journey*. (San Francisco: HarperSanFrancisco, 1993), 69.

3. Ibid., 72.

4. Ibid., 74.

5. Ibid.

6. Jason Aronson Inc., 1996.

## Chapter 8

1. Kate Hood, "Marriage under the Care of the Meeting." *Quaker Life*. June, 2000. Accessed online May, 2005.

2. NCYM Publications Board, *A Wedding After the Manner of Friends*. (Greensboro, NC: NCYM Publications Board, 2000), 13-14.

3. Tom Mullen, "When Friends Say Goodbye." *Quaker Life*. April, 2000.

4. Ibid.

5. Philip Andrew Raines, *The Friendly Rites: Rites of Passage within Quaker Education*. (Term paper, Earlham School of Religion, 2000), 7–11.

## Chapter 9

1. Augustine, "De Catechizandis rudibus" as quoted by Daniel Kennedy in "Sacraments." *The Catholic Encyclopedia*. Vol. 13. (New York: Robert Appleton Company, 1912), 1.

2. J. Bill Ratliff, (Editor). *Out of the Silence: Quaker Perspectives on Pastoral Care and Counseling*. (Wallingford, PA: Pendle Hill Publications, 2001), 10.

3. Ibid., 12.

4. *Merriam-Webster.com*. "Kairos." Accessed August, 2016. http://www.merriam-webster.com/dictionary/kairos.

## Chapter 10

1. Wade Clark Roof, *A Generation of Seekers: The Spiritual Journeys of the Baby Boom Generation.* (San Francisco: HarperSanFrancisco, 1993), 67.

2. Packard N. Brown, "Bivocational Ministry on the Rise." *In Trust*, Vol. 29, No. 3 (Spring): 2018, 16.

3. Pew Research Center: Religion & Public Life. (2015) "Fifteen Largest Protestant Denominations," *Pewforum*. Accessed August, 2018. http://www.pewforum.org/2015/05/12/ chapter-1-the-changing-religious-composition-of-the-u-s/pr_15-05-12_rls_chapter1-03/.

## Appendix

1. NCYM Publications Board, *A Wedding After the Manner of Friends*, 2000. Pages 13-14 reprinted here by permission of original authors, New Garden Friends Meeting.

# BIBLIOGRAPHY

Angell, Stephen W. and Pink Dandelion. *The Oxford Handbook of Quaker Studies*. Oxford: Oxford University Press, 2013.

Barbour, Hugh, and J. William Frost. *The Quakers*. Richmond, IN: Friends United Press, 1988.

Bean, Joel. "The pastoral movement." *The British Friend* 47, No. 1 (January), 1889. Accessed online January, 2009. http://www.qhpress.org/quaker pages/qwhp/pastor.htm.

Boulbie, Judith. *A testimony for truth against all hireling-priests and deceivers: with a cry to the inhabitants of this nation, to turn to the Lord, before his dreadful judgments overtake them. Also a testimony against all observers of times and dayes.* 1665. Electronic Publisher: Earlham School of Religion: Digital Quaker Collection. Book # E27658342. Accessed January 21, 2009. http://dqc.esr.earlham.edu:8080/xmlmm/docButton?XMLMMWhat=zoom&XMLMMWhere=out&XMLMMHitNumber=4&XMLMMBeanName=toc1&XMLMMNextPage=/printHit.jsp&XMLMMXpath.

Bownas, Samuel. *A description of the qualifications necessary to a gospel minister*. Philadelphia: Pendle Hill Publications, 1989.

Brinton, Howard. *Friends for 300 Years*. New York: Harper and Brothers, 1952.

Brown, Ira V. "Pennsylvania's Antislavery Pioneers, 1688-1776." *Pennsylvania History: A Journal of Mid-Atlantic Studies,* Vol. 55, No. 2 (1988). 59–77.

Brown, Packard N. "Bivocational Ministry on the Rise."
*In Trust*, Vol. 29, No. 3 (Spring 2018). 16–17.

Cooper, Wilmer A. *A Living Faith: An Historical Study of
Quaker Beliefs*. Richmond, IN: Friends United Press,
1990.

Edmundson, William. *A journal of the life, travels, sufferings,
and labour of love in the work of the ministry, of that
worthy elder and faithful servant of Jesus Christ,
William Edmundson*. Dublin: Christopher
Bentham, 1820. Electronic Publisher: Earlham
School of Religion: Digital Quaker Collection. Book
#E18970680. Accesssed January, 2009. http://dqc.
esr.earlham.edu:8080/xmlmm/docButton?XMLM-
MWhat=zoom&XMLMMWhere=in&XMLMMHit-
Number=3&XMLMMBeanName=toc1&XM-
LMMNextPage=/printHit.jsp.

Freiday, Dean. *Barclay's Apology in Modern English*. Newberg,
OR: Barclay Press, 1991.

Hamm, Thomas D. *The Quakers in America*. New York:
Columbia University Press, 2003.

Hamm, Thomas D. *The Transformation of American Quakerism: Orthodox Friends, 1800-1907*. Bloomington, IN:
Indiana University Press, 1988.

Hood, Kate. "Marriage under the Care of the Meeting."
*Quaker Life*. June, 2000. Accessed online May, 2005.

Kärkkäinen, Veli-Matti. *An Introduction to Ecclesiology:
Ecumenical, Historical & Global Perspectives*. Downers
Grove, IL: InterVarsity, 2002.

Katz, David and Peter Lovenheim, *Reading Between the
Lines: New Stories from the Bible*. Jason Aronson Inc.,
1996.

St. Augustine, "De Catechizandis rudibus," quoted in
Daniel Kennedy, "Sacraments," *The Catholic Encyclopedia.* Vol. 13. New York: Robert Appleton Company, 1912. Accessed August 26, 2016. http://www.newadvent.org/cathen/13295a.htm.

*Merriam-Webster.com.* "Kairos." Accessed September, 2016. http://www.merriam-webster.com/dictionary/kairos.

Mullen, Tom. "When Friends Say Goodbye." *Quaker Life.* April, 2000. Accessed online January, 2006.

NCYM Publications Board. *A Wedding After the Manner of Friends.* Greensboro, NC: NCYM Publications Board, 2000.

Nickalls, John L. *Journal of George Fox.* Philadelphia: Religious Society of Friends, 1985.

Nouwen, Henri J.M. *In the Name of Jesus: Reflections on Christian Leadership.* New York: Crossroad, 1996.

Palmer, Parker J. *To Know as We Are Known: Education as a Spiritual Journey.* San Francisco: HarperSanFrancisco, 1993.

Pew Research Center: Religion & Public Life. (2015) "Fifteen Largest Protestant Denominations," *Pewforum.* Accessed August, 2018. http://www.pewforum.org/2015/05/12/ chapter-1-the-changing-religious-composition-of-the-u-s/pr_15-05-12_rls_chapter1-03/.

Raines, Philip Andrew. *The Friendly Rites: Rites of Passage within Quaker Education.* Term paper, Earlham School of Religion, 2000.

Ratliff, Richard P. *Our Special Heritage: The Sesquicentennial Publication of Indiana Yearly Meeting of Friends*. New Castle, IN: Community Printing Co., 1970.

Ratliff, J. Bill, ed. *Out of the Silence: Quaker Perspectives on Pastoral Care and Counseling*. Wallingford, PA: Pendle Hill Publications, 2001.

Roof, Wade Clark. *A Generation of Seekers: The Spiritual Journeys of the Baby Boom Generation*. San Francisco: HarperSanFrancisco, 1993.

Thornburg, Stan. "Open worship." *Quaker Life*, Series 38, No. 6 (1997): 20-21.

Trueblood, D. Elton. *The People Called Quakers*. Richmond, IN: Friends United Press, 1971.

Willcuts, Jack L. *Why Friends Are Friends*. Newberg, OR: Barclay Press, 1984.

Wilson, Lloyd Lee. *Essays on the Quaker Vision of Gospel Order*. Philadelphia: Friends General Conference, 2001.

CPSIA information can be obtained
at www.ICGtesting.com
Printed in the USA
FFHW021839140119
50157141-55068FF